STUDIES IN CLASSIC
AMERICAN LITERATURE

BY D. H. LAWRENCE

NOVELS

*Sons and Lovers
*The Rainbow
*Women in Love
*The Lost Girl
*Aaron's Rod
*Kangaroo
 Lady Chatterley's Lover
*Four Short Novels (*Love among the Haystacks,
    The Ladybird, The Fox, The Captain's Doll*)

NONFICTION

*Psychoanalysis and the Unconscious *and*
    Fantasia of the Unconscious
*Studies in Classic American Literature
*Apocalypse
*Sex, Literature and Censorship

COLLECTIONS

 Phoenix
 The Portable D. H. Lawrence
*Selected Poems
*The Complete Short Stories of D. H. Lawrence
*Selected Literary Criticism
 The Collected Letters of D. H. Lawrence
*The Complete Poems of D. H. Lawrence
 The Complete Plays of D. H. Lawrence
*Phoenix II
*D. H. Lawrence and Italy: Twilight in Italy, Sea and
    Sardinia, Etruscan Places

VIKING CRITICAL EDITION

 Sons and Lovers (*edited by Julian Moynahan*)

Available in Viking Compass edition.

D. H. LAWRENCE

Studies in Classic
American Literature

THE VIKING PRESS
NEW YORK

Twelfth printing January 1972

Originally published in 1923 by Thomas Seltzer Inc.
Re-issued in 1964 by The Viking Press, Inc.
625 Madison Avenue, New York, N.Y. 10022
Viking Compass edition issued simultaneously

Published simultaneously in Canada by
The Macmillan Company of Canada Limited

SBN 670-67958-5 (hardbound)
SBN 670-00147-3 (paperbound)

Library of Congress catalog card number: 64-4884

Printed in U.S.A. by the Murray Printing Co.

CONTENTS

FOREWORD

Listen to the States asserting: "The hour has struck! Americans shall be American. The U.S.A. is now grown up artistically. It is time we ceased to hang on to the skirts of Europe, or to behave like schoolboys let loose from European schoolmasters—"

All right, Americans, let's see you set about it. Go on then, let the precious cat out of the bag. If you're sure he's in.

> *Et interrogatum est ab omnibus:*
> *"Ubi est ille Toad-in-the-Hole?"*
> *Et iteratum est ab omnibus:*
> *"Non est inventus!"*

Is he or isn't he inventus?

If he is, of course, he must be somewhere inside you, Oh American. No good chasing him over all the old continents, of course. But equally no good *asserting* him merely. Where *is* this new bird called the true American? Show us the homunculus of the new era. Go on, show us him. Because all that is visible to the naked European eye, in America, is a sort of recreant European. We want to see this missing link of the next era.

Well, we still don't get him. So the only thing to do is to have a look for him under the American bushes. The old American literature, to start with.

"The old American literature! Franklin, Cooper, Hawthorne & Co.? All that mass of words! all so unreal!" cries the live American.

Heaven knows what we mean by reality. Telephone, tinned meat, Charlie Chaplin, water-taps, and World-Salvation, presumably. Some insisting on the plumbing, and some on saving the world: these being the two great American specialties. Why not? Only, what about the young homunculus of the new era, meanwhile? You can't save yourself before you are born.

Look at me trying to be midwife to the unborn homunculus!

Two bodies of modern literature seem to me to have come to a real verge: the Russian and the American. Let us leave aside the more brittle bits of French or Marinetti or Irish production, which are perhaps over the verge. Russian and American. And by American I do not mean Sherwood Anderson, who is so Russian. I mean the old people, little thin volumes of Hawthorne, Poe, Dana, Melville, Whitman. These seem to me to have reached a verge, as the more voluminous Tolstoi, Dostoevsky, Chekhov, Artzibashev reached a limit on the other side. The furthest frenzies of French modernism or futurism have not yet reached the pitch of extreme consciousness that Poe, Melville, Hawthorne, Whitman reached. The European moderns are all *trying* to be extreme. The great Americans I mention just were it. Which is why the world has funked them, and funks them to-day.

The great difference between the extreme Russians and the extreme Americans lies in the fact that the Russians are explicit and hate eloquence and symbols, seeing in these only subterfuge, whereas the Americans refuse everything explicit and always put up a sort of double meaning. They revel in subterfuge. They prefer their truth safely swaddled in an ark of bulrushes, and deposited among the reeds until some friendly Egyptian princess comes to rescue the babe.

Well, it's high time now that someone came to lift out the swaddled infant of truth that America spawned some time back. The child must be getting pretty thin, from neglect.

STUDIES IN CLASSIC
AMERICAN LITERATURE

CHAPTER I

THE SPIRIT OF PLACE

WE like to think of the old-fashioned American classics as children's books. Just childishness, on our part. The old American art-speech contains an alien quality, which belongs to the American continent and to nowhere else. But, of course, so long as we insist on reading the books as children's tales, we miss all that.

One wonders what the proper high-brow Romans of the third and fourth or later centuries read into the strange utterances of Lucretius or Apuleius or Tertullian, Augustine or Athanasius. The uncanny voice of Iberian Spain, the weirdness of old Carthage, the passion of Libya and North Africa; you may bet the proper old Romans never heard these at all. They read old Latin inference over the top of it, as we read old European inference over the top of Poe or Hawthorne.

It is hard to hear a new voice, as hard as it is to listen to an unknown language. We just don't listen. There is a new voice in the old American classics. The world has declined to hear it, and has babbled about children's stories.

Why?—Out of fear. The world fears a new experience more than it fears anything. Because a new experience displaces so many old experiences. And it is like trying to use muscles that have perhaps never been used, or that have been going stiff for ages. It hurts horribly.

The world doesn't fear a new idea. It can pigeon-hole any idea. But it can't pigeon-hole a real new experience. It can only dodge. The world is a great dodger, and the Americans the greatest. Because they dodge their own very selves.

There is a new feeling in the old American books, far more than there is in the modern American books, which are pretty empty of any feeling, and proud of it. There is a "different" feeling in the old American classics. It is the shifting over from the old psyche to something new, a dis-

1

placement. And displacements hurt. This hurts. So we try to tie it up, like a cut finger. Put a rag round it.

It is a cut too. Cutting away the old emotions and consciousness. Don't ask what is left.

Art-speech is the only truth. An artist is usually a damned liar, but his art, if it be art, will tell you the truth of his day. And that is all that matters. Away with eternal truth. Truth lives from day to day, and the marvellous Plato of yesterday is chiefly bosh to-day.

The old American artists were hopeless liars. But they were artists, in spite of themselves. Which is more than you can say of most living practitioners.

And you can please yourself, when you read *The Scarlet Letter*, whether you accept what that sugary, blue-eyed little darling of a Hawthorne has to say for himself, false as all darlings are, or whether you read the impeccable truth of his art-speech.

The curious thing about art-speech is that it prevaricates so terribly, I mean it tells such lies. I suppose because we always all the time tell ourselves lies. And out of a pattern of lies art weaves the truth. Like Dostoevsky posing as a sort of Jesus, but most truthfully revealing himself all the while as a little horror.

Truly art is a sort of subterfuge. But thank God for it, we can see through the subterfuge if we choose. Art has two great functions. First, it provides an emotional experience. And then, if we have the courage of our own feelings, it becomes a mine of practical truth. We have had the feelings *ad nauseam*. But we've never dared dig the actual truth out of them, the truth that concerns us, whether it concerns our grandchildren or not.

The artist usually sets out—or used to—to point a moral and adorn a tale. The tale, however, points the other way, as a rule. Two blankly opposing morals, the artist's and the tale's. Never trust the artist. Trust the tale. The proper function of a critic is to save the tale from the artist who created it.

Now we know our business in these studies; saving the American tale from the American artist.

Let us look at this American artist first. How did he ever get to America, to start with? Why isn't he a European still, like his father before him?

Now listen to me, don't listen to him. He'll tell you the lie you expect. Which is partly your fault for expecting it.

He didn't come in search of freedom of worship. England had more freedom of worship in the year 1700 than America had. Won by Englishmen who wanted freedom, and so stopped at home and fought for it. And got it. Freedom of worship? Read the history of New England during the first century of its existence.

Freedom anyhow? The land of the free! This the land of the free! Why, if I say anything that displeases them, the free mob will lynch me, and that's my freedom. Free? Why, I have never been in any country where the individual has such an abject fear of his fellow countrymen. Because, as I say, they are free to lynch him the moment he shows he is not one of them.

No, no, if you're so fond of the truth about Queen Victoria, try a little about yourself.

Those Pilgrim Fathers and their successors never came here for freedom of worship. What did they set up when they got here? Freedom, would you call it?

They didn't come for freedom. Or if they did, they sadly went back on themselves.

All right then, what did they come for? For lots of reasons. Perhaps least of all in search of freedom of any sort: positive freedom, that is.

They came largely to get *away*—that most simple of motives. To get away. Away from what? In the long run, away from themselves. Away from everything. That's why most people have come to America, and still do come. To get away from everything they are and have been.

"Henceforth be masterless."

Which is all very well, but it isn't freedom. Rather the reverse. A hopeless sort of constraint. It is never freedom till you find something you really *positively want to be*. And people in America have always been shouting about the things they are *not*. Unless, of course, they are millionaires, made or in the making.

And after all there is a positive side to the movement. All that vast flood of human life that has flowed over the Atlantic in ships from Europe to America has not flowed over simply on a tide of revulsion from Europe and from the confinements of the European ways of life. This revulsion was, and still is, I believe, the prime motive in emigration. But there was some cause, even for the revulsion.

It seems as if at times man had a frenzy for getting away from any control of any sort. In Europe the old Christianity was the real master. The Church and the true aristocracy bore the responsibility for the working out of the Christian ideals: a little irregularly, maybe, but responsible nevertheless.

Mastery, kingship, fatherhood had their power destroyed at the time of the Renaissance.

And it was precisely at this moment that the great drift over the Atlantic started. What were men drifting away from? The old authority of Europe? Were they breaking the bonds of authority, and escaping to a new more absolute unrestrainedness? Maybe. But there was more to it.

Liberty is all very well, but men cannot live without masters. There is always a master. And men either live in glad obedience to the master they believe in, or they live in a frictional opposition to the master they wish to undermine. In America this frictional opposition has been the vital factor. It has given the Yankee his kick. Only the continual influx of more servile Europeans has provided America with an obedient labouring class. The true obedience never outlasting the first generation.

But there sits the old master, over in Europe. Like a parent. Somewhere deep in every American heart lies a rebellion against the old parenthood of Europe. Yet no American feels he has completely escaped its mastery. Hence the slow, smouldering patience of American opposition. The slow, smouldering, corrosive obedience to the old master Europe, the unwilling subject, the unremitting opposition.

Whatever else you are, be masterless.

> "Ca Ca Caliban
> Get a new master, be a new man."

Escaped slaves, we might say, people the republics of Liberia or Haiti. Liberia enough! Are we to look at America in the same way? A vast republic of escaped slaves. When you consider the hordes from eastern Europe, you might well say it: a vast republic of escaped slaves. But one dare not say this of the Pilgrim Fathers, and the great old body of idealist Americans, the modern Americans tortured with thought. A vast republic of escaped slaves. Look out, America! And a minority of earnest, self-tortured people.

The masterless.

> "Ca Ca Caliban
> Get a new master, be a new man."

What did the Pilgrim Fathers come for, then, when they came so gruesomely over the black sea? Oh, it was in a black spirit. A black revulsion from Europe, from the old authority of Europe, from kings and bishops and popes. And more. When you look into it, more. They were black, masterful men, they wanted something else. No kings, no bishops maybe. Even no God Almighty. But also, no more of this new "humanity" which followed the Renaissance. None of this new liberty which was to be so pretty in Europe. Something grimmer, by no means free-and-easy.

America has never been easy, and is not easy to-day. Americans have always been at a certain tension. Their liberty is a thing of sheer will, sheer tension: a liberty of THOU SHALT NOT. And it has been so from the first. The land of THOU SHALT NOT. Only the first commandment is: THOU SHALT NOT PRESUME TO BE A MASTER. Hence democracy.

"We are the masterless." That is what the American Eagle shrieks. It's a Hen-Eagle.

The Spaniards refused the post-Renaissance liberty of Europe. And the Spaniards filled most of America. The Yankees, too, refused, refused the post-Renaissance humanism of Europe. First and foremost, they hated masters. But under that, they hated the flowing ease of humour in Europe. At the bottom of the American soul was always a dark suspense, at the bottom of the Spanish-American soul the same. And this dark suspense hated and hates the old European spontaneity, watches it collapse with satisfaction.

Every continent has its own great spirit of place. Every people is polarized in some particular locality, which is home, the homeland. Different places on the face of the earth have different vital effluence, different vibration, different chemical exhalation, different polarity with different stars: call it what you like. But the spirit of place is a great reality. The Nile valley produced not only the corn, but the terrific religions of Egypt. China produces the Chinese, and will go on doing so. The Chinese in San Francisco will in time cease to be Chinese, for America is a great melting-pot.

There was a tremendous polarity in Italy, in the city of Rome. And this seems to have died. For even places die. The Island of Great Britain had a wonderful terrestrial magnetism or polarity of its own, which made the British people. For the moment, this polarity seems to be breaking. Can England die? And what if England dies?

Men are less free than they imagine; ah, far less free. The freest are perhaps least free.

Men are free when they are in a living homeland, not when they are straying and breaking away. Men are free when they are obeying some deep, inward voice of religious belief. Obeying from within. Men are free when they belong to a living, organic, *believing* community, active in fulfilling some unfulfilled, perhaps unrealized purpose. Not when they are escaping to some wild west. The most unfree souls go west, and shout of freedom. Men are freest when they are most unconscious of freedom. The shout is a rattling of chains, always was.

Men are not free when they are doing just what they like. The moment you can do just what you like, there is nothing you care about doing. Men are only free when they are doing what the deepest self likes.

And there is getting down to the deepest self! It takes some diving.

Because the deepest self is way down, and the conscious self is an obstinate monkey. But of one thing we may be sure. If one wants to be free, one has to give up the illusion of doing what one likes, and seek what IT wishes done.

But before you can do what IT likes, you must first break the spell of the old mastery, the old IT.

Perhaps at the Renaissance, when kingship and fatherhood fell, Europe drifted into a very dangerous half-truth: of liberty and equality. Perhaps the men who went to America felt this, and so repudiated the old world together. Went one better than Europe. Liberty in America has meant so far the breaking away from *all* dominion. The true liberty will only begin when Americans discover IT, and proceed possibly to fulfil IT. IT being the deepest *whole* self of man, the self in its wholeness, not idealistic halfness.

That's why the Pilgrim Fathers came to America, then; and that's why we come. Driven by IT. We cannot see that invisible winds carry us, as they carry swarms of locusts, that invisible magnetism brings us as it brings the migrating birds to their unforeknown goal. But it is so. We are not the marvellous choosers and deciders we think we are. IT chooses for us, and decides for us. Unless, of course, we are just escaped slaves, vulgarly cocksure of our ready-made destiny. But if we are living people, in touch with the source, IT drives us and decides us. We are free only so long as we obey. When we run counter, and think we will do as we like, we just flee around like Orestes pursued by the Eumenides.

And still, when the great day begins, when Americans have at last discovered America and their own wholeness, still there will be the vast number of escaped slaves to reckon with, those who have no cocksure, ready-made destinies.

Which will win in America, the escaped slaves, or the new whole men?

The real American day hasn't begun yet. Or at least, not yet sunrise. So far it has been the false dawn. That is, in the progressive American consciousness there has been the one dominant desire, to do away with the old thing. Do away with masters, exalt the will of the people. The will of the people being nothing but a figment, the exalting doesn't count for much. So, in the name of the will of the people, get rid of masters. When you have got rid of masters, you are left with this mere phrase of the will of the people. Then you pause and bethink yourself, and try to recover your own wholeness.

So much for the conscious American motive, and for democracy over here. Democracy in America is just the tool with which the old master of Europe, the European spirit, is undermined. Europe destroyed, potentially, American democracy will evaporate. America will begin.

American consciousness has so far been a false dawn. The negative ideal of democracy. But underneath, and contrary to this open ideal, the first hints and revelations of IT. IT, the American whole soul.

You have got to pull the democratic and idealistic clothes off American utterance, and see what you can of the dusky body of IT underneath.

"Henceforth be masterless."

Henceforth be mastered.

CHAPTER II

BENJAMIN FRANKLIN

THE Perfectibility of Man! Ah heaven, what a dreary theme! The perfectibility of the Ford car! The perfectibility of which man? I am many men. Which of them are you going to perfect? I am not a mechanical contrivance.

Education! Which of the various me's do you propose to educate, and which do you propose to suppress?

Anyhow, I defy you. I defy you, oh society, to educate me or to suppress me, according to your dummy standards.

The ideal man! And which is he, if you please? Benjamin Franklin or Abraham Lincoln? The ideal man! Roosevelt or Porfirio Díaz?

There are other men in me, besides this patient ass who sits here in a tweed jacket. What am I doing, playing the patient ass in a tweed jacket? Who am I talking to? Who are you, at the other end of this patience?

Who are you? How many selves have you? And which of these selves do you want to be?

Is Yale College going to educate the self that is in the dark of you, or Harvard College?

The ideal self! Oh, but I have a strange and fugitive self shut out and howling like a wolf or a coyote under the ideal windows. See his red eyes in the dark? This is the self who is coming into his own.

The perfectibility of man, dear God! When every man as long as he remains alive is in himself a multitude of conflicting men. Which of these do you choose to perfect, at the expense of every other?

Old Daddy Franklin will tell you. He'll rig him up for you, the pattern American. Oh, Franklin was the first downright American. He knew what he was about, the sharp little man. He set up the first dummy American.

At the beginning of his career this cunning little Benjamin drew up for himself a creed that should "satisfy the professors of every religion, but shock none".

9

Now wasn't that a real American thing to do?

"That there is One God, who made all things."

(But Benjamin made Him.)

"That He governs the world by His Providence."

(Benjamin knowing all about Providence.)

"That He ought to be worshipped with adoration, prayer, and thanksgiving."

(Which cost nothing.)

"But——" But me no buts, Benjamin, saith the Lord.

"But that the most acceptable service of God is doing good to men."

(God having no choice in the matter.)

"That the soul is immortal."

(You'll see why, in the next clause.)

"And that God will certainly reward virtue and punish vice, either here or hereafter."

Now if Mr. Andrew Carnegie, or any other millionaire, had wished to invent a God to suit his ends, he could not have done better. Benjamin did it for him in the eighteenth century. God is the supreme servant of men who want to get on, to *produce*. Providence. The provider. The heavenly storekeeper. The everlasting Wanamaker.

And this is all the God the grandsons of the Pilgrim Fathers had left. Aloft on a pillar of dollars.

"That the soul is immortal."

The trite way Benjamin says it!

But man has a soul, though you can't locate it either in his purse or his pocket-book or his heart or his stomach or his head. The *wholeness* of a man is his soul. Not merely that nice little comfortable bit which Benjamin marks out.

It's a queer thing is a man's soul. It is the whole of him. Which means it is the unknown him, as well as the known. It seems to me just funny, professors and Benjamins fixing the functions of the soul. Why, the soul of man is a vast forest, and all Benjamin intended was a neat back garden. And we've all got to fit into his kitchen garden scheme of things. Hail Columbia!

The soul of man is a dark forest. The Hercynian Wood that scared the Romans so, and out of which came the white-skinned hordes of the next civilization.

Who knows what will come out of the soul of man? The

soul of man is a dark vast forest, with wild life in it. Think of Benjamin fencing it off!

Oh, but Benjamin fenced a little tract that he called the soul of man, and proceeded to get it into cultivation. Providence, forsooth! And they think that bit of barbed wire is going to keep us in pound for ever? More fools they.

This is Benjamin's barbed wire fence. He made himself a list of virtues, which he trotted inside like a grey nag in a paddock.

I

TEMPERANCE

Eat not to fulness; drink not to elevation.

2

SILENCE

Speak not but what may benefit others or yourself; avoid trifling conversation.

3

ORDER

Let all your things have their places; let each part of your business have its time.

4

RESOLUTION

Resolve to perform what you ought; perform without fail what you resolve.

5

FRUGALITY

Make no expense but to do good to others or yourself— i.e., waste nothing.

6

INDUSTRY

Lose no time, be always employed in something useful; cut off all unnecessary action.

7

SINCERITY

Use no hurtful deceit; think innocently and justly, and, if you speak, speak accordingly.

8

JUSTICE

Wrong none by doing injuries, or omitting the benefits that are your duty.

9

MODERATION

Avoid extremes, forbear resenting injuries as much as you think they deserve.

10

CLEANLINESS

Tolerate no uncleanliness in body, clothes, or habitation.

11

TRANQUILLITY

Be not disturbed at trifles, or at accidents common or unavoidable.

12

CHASTITY

Rarely use venery but for health and offspring, never to dulness, weakness, or the injury of your own or another's peace or reputation.

13

HUMILITY

Imitate Jesus and Socrates.

A Quaker friend told Franklin that he, Benjamin, was generally considered proud, so Benjamin put in the Humility touch as an afterthought. The amusing part is the sort of humility it displays. "Imitate Jesus and Socrates," and mind you don't outshine either of these two. One can just imagine Socrates and Alcibiades roaring in their cups over Philadelphian Benjamin, and Jesus looking at him a little puzzled, and murmuring: "Aren't you wise in your own conceit, Ben?"

"Henceforth be masterless," retorts Ben. "Be ye each one his own master unto himself, and don't let even the Lord put His spoke in." "Each man his own master" is but a puffing up of masterlessness.

Well, the first of Americans practised this enticing list with assiduity, setting a national example. He had the virtues in columns, and gave himself good and bad marks according as he thought his behaviour deserved. Pity these conduct charts are lost to us. He only remarks that Order was his stumbling block. He could not learn to be neat and tidy.

Isn't it nice to have nothing worse to confess?

He was a little model, was Benjamin. Doctor Franklin. Snuff-coloured little man! Immortal soul and all!

The immortal soul part was a sort of cheap insurance policy.

Benjamin had no concern, really, with the immortal soul. He was too busy with social man.

1. He swept and lighted the streets of young Philadelphia.

2. He invented electrical appliances.

3. He was the centre of a moralizing club in Philadelphia, and he wrote the moral humorisms of Poor Richard.

4. He was a member of all the important councils of Philadelphia, and then of the American colonies.

5. He won the cause of American Independence at the French Court, and was the economic father of the United States.

Now what more can you want of a man? And yet he is *infra dig.*, even in Philadelphia.

I admire him. I admire his sturdy courage first of all, then his sagacity, then his glimpsing into the thunders of electricity, then his common-sense humour. All the qualities of a great man, and never more than a great cititzen. Middle-sized, sturdy, snuff-coloured Doctor Franklin, one of the soundest citizens that ever trod or "used venery".

I do not like him.

And, by the way, I always thought books of Venery were about hunting deer.

There is a certain earnest naïveté about him. Like a child. And like a little old man. He has again become as a little child, always as wise as his grandfather, or wiser.

Perhaps, as I say, the most complete citizen that ever "used venery".

Printer, philosopher, scientist, author and patriot, impeccable husband and citizen, why isn't he an archetype?

Pioneer, Oh Pioneers! Benjamin was one of the greatest pioneers of the United States. Yet we just can't do with him.

What's wrong with him then? Or what's wrong with us?

I can remember, when I was a little boy, my father used to buy a scrubby yearly almanac with the sun and moon and stars on the cover. And it used to prophesy bloodshed and famine. But also crammed in corners it had little anecdotes and humorisms, with a moral tag. And I used to have my little priggish laugh at the woman who counted her chickens before they were hatched and so forth, and I was convinced that honesty was the best policy, also a little priggishly. The author of these bits was Poor Richard, and Poor Richard was Benjamin Franklin, writing in Philadelphia well over a hundred years before.

And probably I haven't got over those Poor Richard tags yet. I rankle still with them. They are thorns in young flesh.

Because, although I still believe that honesty is the best policy, I dislike policy altogether; though it is just as well not to count your chickens before they are hatched, its still more hateful to count them with gloating when they *are* hatched. It has taken me many years and countless smarts to get out of that barbed wire moral enclosure that Poor Richard rigged up. Here am I now in tatters and scratched to ribbons, sitting in the middle of Benjamin's America looking at the barbed wire, and the fat sheep crawling under the fence to get fat outside, and the watch-dogs yelling at the gate lest by chance anyone should get out by the proper exit. Oh America! Oh Benjamin! And I just utter a long loud curse against Benjamin and the American corral.

Moral America! Most moral Benjamin. Sound, satisfied Ben!

He had to go to the frontiers of his State to settle some disturbance among the Indians. On this occasion he writes:

"We found that they had made a great bonfire in the middle of the square; they were all drunk, men and women quarrelling and fighting. Their dark-coloured bodies, half-naked, seen only by the gloomy light of the bonfire, running after and beating one another with fire-brands, accompanied by their horrid yellings, formed a scene the most resembling our ideas of hell that could well be imagined. There was no appeasing the tumult, and we retired to our lodging. At midnight a number of them came thundering at our door, demanding more rum, of which we took no notice.

"The next day, sensible they had misbehaved in giving us that disturbance, they sent three of their counsellors to make their apology. The orator acknowledged the fault, but laid it upon the rum, and then endeavoured to excuse the rum by saying: 'The Great Spirit, who made all things, made everything for some use; and whatever he designed anything for, that use it should always be put to. Now, when he had made the rum, he said: "Let this be for the Indians to get drunk with." And it must be so.'

"And, indeed, if it be the design of Providence to extirpate these savages in order to make room for the cultivators of the earth, it seems not improbable that rum may be the appointed means. It has already annihilated all the tribes who formerly inhabited all the seacoast. . . ."

This, from the good doctor with such suave complacency, is a little disenchanting. Almost too good to be true.

But there you are! The barbed wire fence. "Extirpate these savages in order to make room for the cultivators of the earth." Oh, Benjamin Franklin! He even "used venery" as a cultivator of seed.

Cultivate the earth, ye gods! The Indians did that, as much as they needed. And they left off there. Who built Chicago? Who cultivated the earth until it spawned Pittsburgh, Pa?

The moral issue! Just look at it! Cultivation included.

If it's a mere choice of Kultur or cultivation, I give it up.

Which brings us right back to our question, what's wrong with Benjamin, that we can't stand him? Or else, what's wrong with us, that we find fault with such a paragon?

Man is a moral animal. All right. I am a moral animal. And I'm going to remain such. I'm not going to be turned into a virtuous little automaton as Benjamin would have me. "This is good, that is bad. Turn the little handle and let the good tap flow," saith Benjamin, and all America with him. "But first of all extirpate those savages who are always turning on the bad tap."

I am a moral animal. But I am not a moral machine. I don't work with a little set of handles or levers. The Temperance-silence-order-resolution - frugality - industry - sincerity-justice - moderation - cleanliness - tranquillity - chastity-humility keyboard is not going to get me going. I'm really not just an automatic piano with a moral Benjamin getting tunes out of me.

Here's my creed, against Benjamin's. This is what I believe:

"That I am I."

"That my soul is a dark forest."

"That my known self will never be more than a little clearing in the forest."

"That gods, strange gods, come forth from the forest into the clearing of my known self, and then go back."

"That I must have the courage to let them come and go."

"That I will never let mankind put anything over me, but that I will try always to recognize and submit to the gods in me and the gods in other men and women."

There is my creed. He who runs may read. He who prefers to crawl, or to go by gasoline, can call it rot.

Then for a "list". It is rather fun to play at Benjamin.

I

TEMPERANCE

Eat and carouse with Bacchus, or munch dry bread with Jesus, but don't sit down without one of the gods.

2

SILENCE

Be still when you have nothing to say; when genuine passion moves you, say what you've got to say, and say it hot.

3

ORDER

Know that you are responsible to the gods inside you and to the men in whom the gods are manifest. Recognize your superiors and your inferiors, according to the gods. This is the root of all order.

4

RESOLUTION

Resolve to abide by your own deepest promptings, and to sacrifice the smaller thing to the greater. Kill when you must, and be killed the same: the *must* coming from the gods inside you, or from the men in whom you recognize the Holy Ghost.

5

FRUGALITY

Demand nothing; accept what you see fit. Don't waste your pride or squander your emotion.

6

INDUSTRY

Lose no time with ideals; serve the Holy Ghost; never serve mankind.

7

SINCERITY

To be sincere is to remember that I am I, and that the other man is not me.

8

JUSTICE

The only justice is to follow the sincere intuition of the

soul, angry or gentle. Anger is just, and pity is just, but judgment is never just.

9
MODERATION

Beware of absolutes. There are many gods.

10
CLEANLINESS

Don't be too clean. It impoverishes the blood.

11
TRANQUILLITY

The soul has many motions, many gods come and go. Try and find your deepest issue, in every confusion, and abide by that. Obey the man in whom you recognize the Holy Ghost; command when your honour comes to command.

12
CHASTITY

Never "use" venery at all. Follow your passional impulse, if it be answered in the other being; but never have any motive in mind, neither offspring nor health nor even pleasure, nor even service. Only know that "venery" is of the great gods. An offering-up of yourself to the very great gods, the dark ones, and nothing else.

13
HUMILITY

See all men and women according to the Holy Ghost that is within them. Never yield before the barren.

There's my list. I have been trying dimly to realize it for a long time, and only America and old Benjamin have at last goaded me into trying to formulate it.

And now I, at least, know why I can't stand Benjamin. He tries to take away my wholeness and my dark forest, my freedom. For how can any man be free, without an illimitable background? And Benjamin tries to shove me into a barbed wire paddock and make me grow potatoes or Chicagoes.

And how can I be free, without gods that come and go? But Benjamin won't let anything exist except my useful fellow men, and I'm sick of them; as for his Godhead, his Providence, He is Head of nothing except a vast heavenly store that keeps every imaginable line of goods, from victrolas to cat-o'-nine tails.

And how can any man be free without a soul of his own, that he believes in and won't sell at any price? But Benjamin doesn't let me have a soul of my own. He says I am nothing but a servant of mankind—galley-slave I call it—and if I don't get my wages here below—that is, if Mr. Pierpont Morgan or Mr. Nosey Hebrew or the grand United States Government, the great US, US or SOMEOFUS, manages to scoop in my bit, along with their lump—why, never mind, I shall get my wages HEREAFTER.

Oh Benjamin! Oh Binjum! You do NOT suck me in any longer.

And why, oh why should the snuff-coloured little trap have wanted to take us all in? Why did he do it?

Out of sheer human cussedness, in the first place. We do all like to get things inside a barbed wire corral. Especially our fellow men. We love to round them up inside the barbed wire enclosure of FREEDOM, and make 'em work. "*Work, you free jewel, WORK!*" shouts the liberator, cracking his whip. Benjamin, I will not work. I do not choose to be a free democrat. I am absolutely a servant of my own Holy Ghost.

Sheer cussedness! But there was as well the salt of a subtler purpose. Benjamin was just in his eyeholes—to use an English vulgarism, meaning he was just delighted—when he was at Paris judiciously milking money out of the French monarchy for the overthrow of all monarchy. If you want to ride your horse to somewhere you must put a bit in his mouth. And Benjamin wanted to ride his horse so that it would upset the whole apple-cart of the old masters. He wanted the whole European apple-cart upset. So he had to put a strong bit in the mouth of his ass.

"Henceforth be masterless."

That is, he had to break-in the human ass completely, so that much more might be broken, in the long run. For the moment it was the British Government that had to have a hole knocked in it. The first real hole it ever had: the breach of the American rebellion.

Benjamin, in his sagacity, knew that the breaking of the old world was a long process. In the depths of his own under-consciousness he hated England, he hated Europe, he hated the whole corpus of the European being. He wanted to be American. But you can't change your nature and mode of consciousness like changing your shoes. It is a gradual shedding. Years must go by, and centuries must elapse before you have finished. Like a son escaping from the domination of his parents. The escape is not just one rupture. It is a long and half-secret process.

So with the American. He was a European when he first went over the Atlantic. He is in the main a recreant European still. From Benjamin Franklin to Woodrow Wilson may be a long stride, but it is a stride along the same road. There is no new road. The same old road, become dreary and futile. Theoretic and materialistic.

Why then did Benjamin set up this dummy of a perfect citizen as a pattern to America? Of course, he did it in perfect good faith, as far as he knew. He thought it simply was the true ideal. But what we *think* we do is not very important. We never really know what we are doing. Either we are materialistic instruments, like Benjamin, or we move in the gesture of creation, from our deepest self, usually unconscious. We are only the actors, we are never wholly the authors of our own deeds or works. IT is the author, the unknown inside us or outside us. The best we can do is to try to hold ourselves in unison with the deeps which are inside us. And the worst we can do is to try to have things our own way, when we run counter to IT, and in the long run get our knuckles rapped for our presumption.

So Benjamin contriving money out of the Court of France. He was contriving the first steps of the overthrow of all Europe, France included. You can never have a new thing without breaking an old. Europe happens to be the old thing. America, unless the people in America assert themselves too much in opposition to the inner gods, should be the new thing. The new thing is the death of the old. But you can't cut the throat of an epoch. You've got to steal the life from it through several centuries.

And Benjamin worked for this both directly and indirectly. Directly, at the Court of France, making a small but very dangerous hole in the side of England, through which hole Europe has by now almost bled to death. And indirectly in Philadelphia, setting up this unlovely, snuff-coloured little ideal, or automaton, of a pattern American. The pattern American, this dry, moral, utilitarian little democrat, has done more to ruin the old Europe than any Russian nihilist. He has done it by slow attrition, like a son who has stayed at home and obeyed his parents, all the while silently hating their authority, and silently, in his soul, destroying not only their authority but their whole existence. For the American spiritually stayed at home in Europe. The spiritual home of America was, and still is, Europe. This is the galling bondage, in spite of several billions of heaped-up gold. Your heaps of gold are only so many muck-heaps, America, and will remain so till you become a reality to yourselves.

All this Americanizing and mechanizing has been for the purpose of overthrowing the past. And now look at America, tangled in her own barbed wire, and mastered by her own machines. Absolutely got down by her own barbed wire of shalt-nots, and shut up fast in her own "productive" machines like millions of squirrels running in millions of cages. It is just a farce.

Now is your chance, Europe. Now let Hell loose and get your own back, and paddle your own canoe on a new sea, while clever America lies on her muck-heaps of gold, strangled in her own barbed wire of shalt-not ideals and shalt-not moralisms. While she goes out to work like millions of squirrels in millions of cages. Production!

Let Hell loose, and get your own back, Europe!

CHAPTER III

HECTOR ST. JOHN DE CRÈVECŒUR

CRÈVECŒUR was born in France, at Caen, in the year 1735. As a boy he was sent over to England and received part of his education there. He went to Canada as a young man, served for a time with Montcalm in the war against the English, and later passed over into the United States, to become an exuberant American. He married a New England girl, and settled on the frontier. During the period of his "cultivating the earth" he wrote the *Letters from an American Farmer*, which enjoyed great vogue in their day, in England especially, among the new reformers like Godwin and Tom Paine.

But Crèvecœur was not a mere cultivator of the earth. That was his best stunt, shall we say. He himself was more concerned with a perfect society and his own manipulation thereof, than with growing carrots. Behold him, then, trotting off importantly and idealistically to France, leaving his farm in the wilds to be burnt by the Indians, and his wife to shift as best she might. This was during the American War of Independence, when the Noble Red Man took to behaving like his own old self. On his return to America, the American Farmer entered into public affairs and into commerce. Again tripping to France, he enjoyed himself as a littérateur Child-of-Nature-sweet-and-pure, was a friend of old Benjamin Franklin in Paris, and quite a favourite with Jean Jacques Rousseau's Madame d'Houdetot, that literary soul.

Hazlitt, Godwin, Shelley, Coleridge, the English romanticists, were, of course, thrilled by the *Letters from an American Farmer*. A new world, a world of the Noble Savage and Pristine Nature and Paradisal Simplicity and all that gorgeousness that flows out of the unsullied fount of the ink-bottle. Lucky Coleridge, who got no farther than Bristol. Some of us have gone all the way.

I think this wild and noble America is the thing that I have pined for most ever since I read Fenimore Cooper, as a boy. Now I've got it.

Franklin is the real *practical* prototype of the American. Crèvecœur is the emotional. To the European, the American is first and foremost a dollar-fiend. We tend to forget the emotional heritage of Hector St. John de Crèvecœur. We tend to disbelieve, for example, in Woodrow Wilson's wrung heart and wet hanky. Yet surely these are real enough. Aren't they?

It wasn't to be expected that the dry little snuff-coloured Doctor should have it all his own way. The new Americans might use venery for health or offspring, and their time for cultivating potatoes and Chicagoes, but they had got *some* sap in their veins after all. They had got to get a bit of luscious emotion somewhere.

NATURE.

I wish I could write it larger than that.

N A T U R E .

Benjamin overlooked NATURE. But the French Crèvecœur spotted it long before Thoreau and Emerson worked it up. Absolutely the safest thing to get your emotional reactions over is NATURE.

Crèvecœur's *Letters* are written in a spirit of touching simplicity, almost better than Chateaubriand. You'd think neither of them would ever know how many beans make five. This American Farmer tells of the joys of creating a home in the wilderness, and of cultivating the virgin soil. Poor virgin, prostituted from the very start.

The Farmer had an Amiable Spouse and an Infant Son, his progeny. He took the Infant Son—who enjoys no other name than this—

> "What is thy name?
> I have no name.
> I am the Infant Son———"

to the fields with him, and seated the same I. S. on the shafts of the plough whilst he, the American Farmer, ploughed the potato patch. He also, the A. F., helped his Neighbours, whom no doubt he loved as himself, to build a barn, and they laboured together in the Innocent

Simplicity of one of Nature's Communities. Meanwhile the Amiable Spouse, who likewise in Blakean simplicity has No Name, cooked the dough-nuts or the pie, though these are not mentioned. No doubt she was a deep-breasted daughter of America, though she may equally well have been a flat-bosomed Methodist. She would have been an Amiable Spouse in either case, and the American Farmer asked no more. I don't know whether her name was Lizzie or Ahoolibah, and probably Crèvecœur didn't. Spouse was enough for him. "Spouse, hand me the carving knife."

The Infant Son developed into Healthy Offspring as more appeared: no doubt Crèvecœur had used venery as directed. And so these Children of Nature toiled in the Wilds at Simple Toil with a little Honest Sweat now and then. You have the complete picture, dear reader. The American Farmer made his own Family Picture, and it is still on view. Of course the Amiable Spouse put on her best apron to be *Im Bild*, for all the world to see and admire.

I used to admire my head off: before I tiptoed into the Wilds and saw the shacks of the Homesteaders. Particularly the Amiable Spouse, poor thing. No wonder *she* never sang the song of Simple Toil in the Innocent Wilds. Poor haggard drudge, like a ghost wailing in the wilderness, nine times out of ten.

Hector St. John, you have lied to me. You lied even more scurrilously to yourself. Hector St. John, you are an emotional liar.

Jean Jacques, Bernardin de St. Pierre, Chateaubriand, exquisite François Le Vaillant, you lying little lot, with your Nature-Sweet-and-Pure! Marie Antoinette got her head off for playing dairy-maid, and nobody even dusted the seats of your pants, till now, for all the lies you put over us.

But Crèvecœur was an artist as well as a liar, otherwise we would not have bothered with him. He wanted to put NATURE in his pocket, as Benjamin put the Human Being. Between them, they wanted the whole scheme of things in their pockets, and the things themselves as well. Once you've got the scheme of things in your pocket, you can do as you like with it, even make money out of it, if you can't find in your heart to destroy it, as was your first intention. So H. St. J. de C. tried to put Nature-Sweet-and-Pure in his pocket. But nature wasn't having any, she poked her head out and baa-ed.

This Nature-sweet-and-pure business is only another effort at intellectualizing. Just an attempt to make all nature succumb to a few laws of the human mind. The sweet-and-pure sort of laws. Nature seemed to be behaving quite nicely, for a while. She has left off.

That's why you get the purest intellectuals in a Garden Suburb or a Brook Farm experiment. You bet, Robinson Crusoe was a high-brow of high-brows.

You can idealize or intellectualize. Or, on the contrary, you can let the dark soul in you see for itself. An artist usually intellectualizes on top, and his dark under-consciousness goes on contradicting him beneath. This is almost laughably the case with most American artists. Crèvecœur is the first example. He is something of an artist, Franklin isn't anything.

Crèvecœur the idealist puts over us a lot of stuff about nature and the noble savage and the innocence of toil, etc., etc. Blarney! But Crèvecœur the artist gives us glimpses of actual nature, not writ large,

Curious that his vision sees only the lowest forms of natural life. Insects, snakes and birds he glimpses in their own mystery, their own pristine being. And straightway gives the lie to Innocent Nature.

"I am astonished to see," he writes quite early in the *Letters*, "that nothing exists but what has its enemy, one species pursue and live upon the other: unfortunately our kingbirds are the destroyers of those industrious insects [the bees]; but on the other hand, these birds preserve our fields from the depredation of crows, which they pursue on the wing with great vigilance and astonishing dexterity."

This is a sad blow to the sweet-and-pureness of Nature. But it is the voice of the artist in contrast to the voice of the ideal turtle. It is the rudimentary American vision. The glimpsing of the king-birds in winged hostility and pride is no doubt the aboriginal Indian vision carrying over. The Eagle symbol in human consciousness. Dark, swinging wings of hawk-beaked destiny, that one cannot help but feel, beating here above the wild centre of America. You look round in vain for the "One being Who made all things, and governs the world by His Providence".

"One species pursue and live upon another."

Reconcile the two statements if you like. But, in America, act on Crèvecœur's observation.

The horse, however, says Hector, is the friend of man, and man is the friend of the horse. But then we leave the horse no choice. And I don't see much *friend*, exactly, in my sly old Indian pony, though he is quite a decent old bird.

Man, too, says Hector, is the friend of man. Whereupon the Indians burnt his farm; so he refrains from mentioning it in the *Letters*, for fear of invalidating his premises.

Some great hornets have fixed their nest on the ceiling of the living-room of the American Farmer, and these tiger-striped animals fly round the heads of the Healthy Offspring and the Amiable Spouse, to the gratification of the American Farmer. He liked their buzz and their tiger waspishness. Also, on the utilitarian plane, they kept the house free of flies. So Hector says. Therefore Benjamin would have approved. But of the feelings of the Amiable S., on this matter, we are not told, and after all, it was she who had to make the jam.

Another anecdote. Swallows built their nest on the veranda of the American Farm. Wrens took a fancy to the nest of the swallows. They pugnaciously (I like the word pugnaciously, it is so American) attacked the harbingers of spring, and drove them away from their nice adobe nest. The swallows returned upon opportunity. But the wrens, coming home, violently drove them forth again. Which continued until the gentle swallows patiently set about to build another nest, while the wrens sat in triumph in the usurped home. The American Farmer watched this contest with delight, and no doubt loudly applauded those little rascals of wrens. For in the Land of the Free, the greatest delight of every man is in getting the better of the other man.

Crèvecœur says he shot a king-bird that had been devouring his bees. He opened the craw and took out a vast number of bees, which little democrats, after they had lain a minute or two stunned, in the sun roused, revived, preened their wings and walked off debonair, like Jonah up the seashore; or like true Yanks escaped from the craw of the king-bird of Europe.

I don't care whether it's true or not. I like the picture, and see in it a parable of the American resurrection.

The humming-bird.

"Its bill is as long and as sharp as a coarse sewing-needle; like the bee, nature has taught it to find out in the calyx of flowers and blossoms those mellifluous particles that can serve it for sufficient food; and yet it seems to leave them untouched, undeprived of anything that our eyes can possibly distinguish. Where it feeds it appears as if immovable, though continually on the wing: and sometimes, from what motives I know not, it will tear and lacerate flowers into a hundred pieces; for, strange to tell, they are the most irascible of the feathered tribe. Where do passions find room in so diminutive a body? They often fight with the fury of lions, until one of the combatants falls a sacrifice and dies. When fatigued, it has often perched within a few feet of me, and on such favourable opportunities I have surveyed it with the most minute attention. Its little eyes appear like diamonds, reflecting light on every side; most elegantly finished in all parts, it is a miniature work of our great parent, who seems to have formed it smallest, and at the same time the most beautiful, of the winged species."

A regular little Tartar, too. Lions no bigger than ink-spots! I have read about humming-birds elsewhere, in Bates and W. H. Hudson, for example. But it is left to the American Farmer to show me the real little raging lion. Birds are evidently no angels in America, or to the true American. He sees how they start and flash their wings like little devils, and stab each other with egoistic sharp bills. But he sees also the reserved, tender shyness of the wild creature, upon occasion. Quails in winter, for instance.

"Often, in the angles of the fences, where the motion of the wind prevents the snow from settling, I carry them both chaff and grain; the one to feed them, the other to prevent their tender feet from freezing fast to the earth, as I have frequently observed them to do."

This is beautiful, and blood-knowledge. Crèvecœur knows the touch of birds' feet, as if they had stood with their vibrating, sharp, cold-cleaving balance, naked-footed on his naked hand. It is a beautiful, barbaric tenderness of the blood. He doesn't after all turn them into "little sisters of the air", like St. Francis, or start preaching to them. He knows them as strange, shy, hot-blooded concentrations of bird-presence.

The *Letter* about snakes and humming-birds is a fine essay, in its primal, dark veracity. The description of the fight between two snakes, a great water-snake and a large black serpent, follows the description of the humming-bird: "Strange was this to behold; two great snakes strongly adhering to the ground, mutually fastened together by means of the writhings which lashed them to each other, and stretched at their full length, they pulled, but pulled in vain; and in the moments of greatest exertions that part of their bodies which was entwined seemed extremely small, while the rest appeared inflated, and now and then convulsed with strong undulations, rapidly following each other. Their eyes seemed on fire, and ready to start out of their heads; at one time the conflict seemed decided; the water-snake bent itself into two great folds, and by that operation rendered the other more than commonly outstretched. The next minute the new struggles of the black one gained an unexpected superiority; it acquired two great folds likewise, which necessarily extended the body of its adversary in proportion as it had contracted its own."

This fight, which Crèvecœur describes to a finish, he calls a sight "uncommon and beautiful". He forgets the sweet-and-pureness of Nature, and is for the time a sheer ophiolater, and his chapter is as handsome a piece of ophiolatry, perhaps, as that coiled Aztec rattlesnake carved in stone.

And yet the real Crèvecœur is, in the issue, neither farmer, nor child of Nature, nor ophiolater. He goes back to France, and figures in the literary salons, and is a friend of Rousseau's Madame d'Houdetot. Also he is a good business man, and arranges a line of shipping between France and America. It all ends in materialism, really. But the *Letters* tell us nothing about this.

We are left to imagine him retiring in grief to dwell with his Red Brothers under the wigwams. For the War of Independence has broken out, and the Indians are armed by the adversaries; they do dreadful work on the frontiers. While

Crèvecœur is away in France his farm is destroyed, his family rendered homeless. So that the last letter laments bitterly over the war, and man's folly and inhumanity to man.

But Crèvecœur ends his lament on a note of resolution. With his amiable spouse, and his healthy offspring, now rising in stature, he will leave the civilized coasts, where man is sophisticated, and therefore inclined to be vile, and he will go to live with the Children of Nature, the Red Men, under the wigwam. No doubt, in actual life, Crèvecœur made some distinction between the Indians who drank rum à la Franklin, and who burnt homesteads and massacred families, and those Indians, the noble Children of Nature, who peopled his own predetermined fancy. Whatever he did in actual life, in his innermost self he would not give up this self-made world, where the natural man was an object of undefiled brotherliness. Touchingly and vividly he describes his tented home near the Indian village, how he breaks the aboriginal earth to produce a little maize, while his wife weaves within the wigwam. And his imaginary efforts to save his tender offspring from the brutishness of unchristian darkness are touching and puzzling, for how can Nature, so sweet and pure under the greenwood tree, how can it have any contaminating effect?

But it is all a swindle. Crèvecœur was off to France in high-heeled shoes and embroidered waistcoat, to pose as a literary man, and to prosper in the world. We, however, must perforce follow him into the backwoods, where the simple natural life shall be perfected, near the tented village of the Red Man.

He wanted, of course, to imagine the dark, savage way of life, to get it all off pat in his head. He wanted to know as the Indians and savages know, darkly, and in terms of otherness. He was simply crazy, as the Americans say, for this. Crazy enough! For at the same time he was absolutely determined that Nature is sweet and pure, that all men are brothers, and equal, and that they love one another like so many cooing doves. He was determined to have life according to his own prescription. Therefore, he wisely kept away from any too close contact with Nature, and took refuge in commerce and the material world. But yet, he was determined to know the savage way of life, to his own *mind's* satisfaction. So he just faked us the last *Letters*. A sort of wish-fulfilment.

For the animals and savages are isolate, each one in its own pristine self. The animal lifts its head, sniffs, and knows within the dark, passionate belly. It knows at once, in dark mindlessness. And at once it flees in immediate recoil; or it crouches predatory, in the mysterious storm of exultant anticipation of seizing a victim; or it lowers its head in blank indifference again; or it advances in the insatiable wild curiosity, insatiable passion to approach that which is unspeakably strange and incalculable; or it draws near in the slow trust of wild, sensual love.

Crèvecœur wanted this kind of knowledge. But comfortably, in his head, along with his other ideas and ideals. He didn't go too near the wigwam. Because he must have suspected that the moment he saw as the savages saw, all his fraternity and equality would go up in smoke, and his ideal world of pure sweet goodness along with it. And still worse than this, he would have to give up his own will, which insists that the world is so, because it would be nicest if it were so. Therefore he trotted back to France in high-heeled shoes, and imagined America in Paris.

He wanted his ideal state. At the same time he wanted to know the other state, the dark, savage mind. He wanted both.

Can't be done, Hector. The one is the death of the other.

Best turn to commerce, where you may get things your own way.

He hates the dark, pre-mental life, really. He hates the true sensual mystery. But he wants to "know". To KNOW. Oh, insatiable American curiosity!

He's a liar.

But if he won't risk knowing in flesh and blood, he'll risk all the imagination you like.

It is amusing to see him staying away and calculating the dangers of the step which he takes so luxuriously, in his fancy, alone. He tickles his palate with a taste of true wildness, as men are so fond nowadays of tickling their palates with a taste of imaginary wickedness—just self-provoked.

"I must tell you," he says, "that there is something in the proximity of the woods which is very singular. It is with men as it is with the plants and animals that grow and live in the forests; they are entirely different from those that live in the plains. I will candidly tell you all my thoughts, but you are not to expect that I shall advance any reasons. By living in or near the woods, their actions are regulated by the wildness of the neighbourhood. The deer often come to eat their grain, the wolves to destroy their sheep, the bears to kill their hogs, the foxes to catch their poultry. This surrounding hostility immediately puts the gun into their hands; they watch these animals, they kill some; and thus by defending their property they soon become professed hunters; this is the progress; once hunters, farewell to the plough. The chase renders them ferocious, gloomy, and unsociable; a hunter wants no neighbour, he rather hates them, because he dreads the competition. . . . Eating of wild meat, whatever you may think, tends to alter their temper. . . ."

Crèvecœur, of course, had never intended to return as a *hunter* to the bosom of Nature, only as a husbandman. The hunter is a killer. The husbandman, on the other hand, brings about the birth and increase. But even the husbandman strains in dark mastery over the unwilling earth and beast; he struggles to win forth substance, he must master the soil and the strong cattle, he must have the heavy blood-knowledge, and the slow, but deep, mastery. There is no equality or selfless humility. The toiling blood swamps the idea, inevitably. For this reason the most idealist nations invent most machines. America simply teems with mechanical inventions, because nobody in America ever wants to *do* anything. They are idealists. Let a machine do the doing.

Again, Crèvecœur dwells on "the apprehension lest my younger children should be caught by that singular charm, so dangerous at their tender years"—meaning the charm of savage life. So he goes on: "By what power does it come to pass that children who have been adopted when young among these people [the Indians] can never be prevailed upon to readopt European manners? Many an anxious parent I have seen last war who, at the return of the peace, went to the Indian villages where they knew their children had been carried in captivity, when to their inexpressible sorrow they found them so perfectly Indianized that many knew them no longer, and those whose more advanced ages permitted them to recollect their fathers and mothers, absolutely refused to follow them, and ran to their adopted parents to protect them against the effusions of love their unhappy real parents lavished on them! Incredible as this may appear, I have heard it asserted in a thousand instances, among persons of credit.

"There must be in their (the Indians') social bond something singularly captivating, and far superior to anything to be boasted of among us; for thousands of Europeans are Indians, and we have no examples of even one of those Aborigines having from choice become Europeans. . . ."

Our cat and another, Hector.

I like the picture of thousands of obdurate offspring, with faces averted from their natural white father and mother, turning resolutely to the Indians of their adoption.

I have seen some Indians whom you really couldn't tell from white men. And I have never seen a white man who looked really like an Indian. So Hector is again a liar.

But Crèvecœur wanted to be an *intellectual* savage, like a great many more we have met. Sweet children of Nature. Savage and bloodthirsty children of Nature.

White Americans do try hard to intellectualize themselves. Especially white women Americans. And the latest stunt is this "savage" stunt again.

White savages, with motor-cars, telephones, incomes and ideals! Savages fast inside the machine; yet savage enough, ye gods!

CHAPTER IV

FENIMORE COOPER'S WHITE NOVELS

BENJAMIN FRANKLIN had a specious little equation in providential mathematics:

$$\text{Rum} + \text{Savage} = 0.$$

Awfully nice! You might add up the universe to nought, if you kept on.

Rum plus Savage may equal a dead savage. But is a dead savage nought? Can you make a land virgin by killing off its aborigines?

The Aztec is gone, and the Incas. The Red Indian, the Esquimo, the Patagonian are reduced to negligible numbers.

Où sont les neiges d'antan?

My dear, wherever they are, they will come down again next winter, sure as houses.

Not that the Red Indian will ever possess the broad lands of America. At least I presume not. But his ghost will.

The Red Man died hating the white man. What remnant of him lives, lives hating the white man. Go near the Indians, and you just feel it. As far as we are concerned, the Red Man is subtly and unremittingly diabolic. Even when he doesn't know it. He is dispossessed in life, and unforgiving. He doesn't believe in us and our civilization, and so is our mystic enemy, for we push him off the face of the earth.

Belief is a mysterious thing. It is the only healer of the soul's wounds. There is no belief in the world.

The Red Man is dead, disbelieving in us. He is dead and unappeased. Do not imagine him happy in his Happy Hunting Ground. No. Only those that die in belief die happy. Those that are pushed out of life in chagrin come back unappeased, for revenge.

A curious thing about the Spirit of Place is the fact that no place exerts its full influence upon a new-comer until the old inhabitant is dead or absorbed. So America. While

the Red Indian existed in fairly large numbers, the new
colonials were in a great measure immune from the daimon,
or demon, of America. The moment the last nuclei of Red
life break up in America, then the white men will have to
reckon with the full force of the demon of the continent.
At present the demon of the place and the unappeased
ghosts of the dead Indians act within the unconscious or
under-conscious soul of the white American, causing the
great American grouch, the Orestes-like frenzy of restless-
ness in the Yankee soul, the inner malaise which amounts
almost to madness, sometimes. The Mexican is macabre
and disintegrated in his own way. Up till now, the
unexpressed spirit of America has worked covertly in the
American, the white American soul. But within the present
generation the surviving Red Indians are due to merge in
the great white swamp. Then the Daimon of America will
work overtly, and we shall see real changes.

There has been all the time, in the white American soul,
a dual feeling about the Indian. First was Franklin's feeling,
that a wise Providence no doubt intended the extirpation of
these savages. Then came Crèvecœur's contradictory feeling
about the noble Red Man and the innocent life of the wigwam. Now we hate to subscribe to Benjamin's belief in a
Providence that wisely extirpates the Indian to make room
for "cultivators of the soil". In Crèvecœur we meet a sentimental desire for the glorification of the savages. Absolutely
sentimental. Hector pops over to Paris to enthuse about the
wigwam.

The desire to extirpate the Indian. And the contradictory
desire to glorify him. Both are rampant still, to-day.

The bulk of the white people who live in contact with
the Indian to-day would like to see this Red brother exter-
minated; not only for the sake of grabbing his land, but
because of the silent, invisible, but deadly hostility between
the spirit of the two races. The minority of whites intellectualize the Red Man and laud him to the skies. But this
minority of whites is mostly a high-brow minority with
a big grouch against its own whiteness. So there you
are.

I doubt if there is possible any real reconciliation, in the
flesh, between the white and the red. For instance, a Red
Indian girl who is servant in the white man's home, if she

is treated with natural consideration, will probably serve well, even happily. She is happy with the new power over the white woman's kitchen. The white world makes her feel prouder, so long as she is free to go back to her own people at the given times. But she is happy because she is playing at being a white woman. There are other Indian women who would never serve the white people, and who would rather die than have a white man for a lover.

In either case, there is no reconciliation. There is no mystic conjunction between the spirit of the two races. The Indian girl who happily serves white people leaves out her own race-consideration, for the time being.

Supposing a white man goes out hunting in the mountains with an Indian. The two will probably get on like brothers. But let the same white man go alone with two Indians, and there will start a most subtle persecution of the unsuspecting white. If they, the Indians, discover that he has a natural fear of steep places, then over every precipice in the country will the trail lead. And so on. Malice! That is the basic feeling in the Indian heart, towards the white. It may even be purely unconscious.

Supposing an Indian loves a white woman, and lives with her. He will probably be very proud of it, for he will be a big man among his own people, especially if the white mistress has money. He will never get over the feeling of pride at dining in a white dining-room and smoking in a white drawing-room. But at the same time he will subtly jeer at his white mistress, try to destroy her white pride. He will submit to her, if he is forced to, with a kind of false, unwilling childishness, and even love her with the same childlike gentleness, sometimes beautiful. But at the bottom of his heart he is gibing, gibing, gibing at her. Not only is it the sex resistance, but the race resistance as well.

There seems to be no reconciliation in the flesh.

That leaves us only expiation, and then reconciliation in the soul. Some strange atonement: expiation and oneing.

Fenimore Cooper has probably done more than any writer to present the Red Man to the white man. But Cooper's presentment is indeed a wish-fulfilment. That is why Fenimore is such a success still.

Modern critics begrudge Cooper his success. I think I resent it a little myself. This popular wish-fulfilment stuff makes it so hard for the real thing to come through, later.

Cooper was a rich American of good family. His father founded Cooperstown, by Lake Champlain. And Fenimore was a gentleman of culture. No denying it.

It is amazing how cultured these Americans of the first half of the eighteenth century were. Most intensely so. Austin Dobson and Andrew Lang are flea-bites in comparison. Volumes of very *raffiné* light verse and finely drawn familiar literature will prove it to anyone who cares to commit himself to these elderly books. The English and French writers of the same period were clumsy and hoydenish, judged by the same standards.

Truly, European decadence was anticipated in America; and American influence passed over to Europe, was assimilated there, and then returned to this land of innocence as something purplish in its modernity and a little wicked. So absurd things are.

Cooper quotes a Frenchman, who says, *"L'Amérique est pourrie avant d'être mûre."* And there is a great deal in it. America was not taught by France—by Baudelaire, for example. Baudelaire learned his lesson from America.

Cooper's novels fall into two classes: his white novels, such as *Homeward Bound*, *Eve Effingham*, *The Spy*, *The Pilot*, and then the *Leatherstocking Series*. Let us look at the white novels first.

The Effinghams are three extremely refined, genteel Americans who are "Homeward Bound" from England to the States. Their party consists of father, daughter, and uncle, and faithful nurse. The daughter has just finished her education in Europe. She has, indeed, skimmed the cream off Europe. England, France, Italy, and Germany have nothing more to teach her. She is bright and charming, admirable creature; a real modern heroine; intrepid, calm, and self-collected, yet admirably impulsive, always in perfectly good taste; clever and assured in her speech, like a man, but withal charmingly deferential and modest before the stronger sex. It is the perfection of the ideal female. We have learned to shudder at her, but Cooper still admired.

On board is the other type of American, the parvenu, the demagogue, who has "done" Europe and put it in his breeches pocket, in a month. Oh, Septimus Dodge, if a European had drawn you, that European would never have been forgiven by America. But an American drew you, so Americans wisely ignore you.

Septimus is the American self-made man. God had no hand in his make-up. He made himself. He has been to Europe, no doubt seen everything, including the Venus de Milo. "What, is *that* the Venus de Milo?" And he turns his back on the lady. He's seen her. He's got her. She's a fish he has hooked, and he's off to America with her, leaving the scum of a statue standing in the Louvre.

That is one American way of Vandalism. The original Vandals would have given the complacent dame a knock with a battle-axe, and ended her. The insatiable American looks at her. "Is *that* the Venus de Milo?—come on!" And the Venus de Milo stands there like a naked slave in a market-place, whom someone has spat on. Spat on!

I have often thought, hearing American tourists in Europe—in the Bargello in Florence, for example, or in the Piazza di San Marco in Venice—exclaiming, "Isn't that just too cunning!" or else, "Aren't you perfectly crazy about Saint Mark's! Don't you think those cupolas are like the loveliest *turnips* upside down, you know"—as if the beautiful things of Europe were just having their guts pulled out by these American admirers. They admire so wholesale. Sometimes they even seem to grovel. But the golden cupolas of St. Mark's in Venice are turnips upside down in a stale stew, after enough American tourists have looked at them. Turnips upside down in a stale stew. Poor Europe!

And there you are. When a few German bombs fell upon Rheims Cathedral up went a howl of execration. But there are more ways than one of vandalism. I should think the American admiration of five-minutes tourists has done more to kill the sacredness of old European beauty and aspiration than multitudes of bombs would have done.

But there you are. Europe has got to fall, and peace hath her victories.

Behold then Mr. Septimus Dodge returning to Dodge-town victorious. Not crowned with laurel, it is true, but wreathed in lists of things he has seen and sucked dry. Seen and sucked dry, you know: Venus de Milo, the Rhine or the Coliseum: swallowed like so many clams, and left the shells.

Now the aristocratic Effinghams, Homeward Bound from

Europe to America, are at the mercy of Mr. Dodge: Septimus. He is their compatriot, so they may not disown him. Had they been English, of course, they would never once have let themselves become aware of his existence. But no. They are American democrats, and therefore, if Mr. Dodge marches up and says: "Mr. Effingham? Pleased to meet you, Mr. Effingham"—why, then Mr. Effingham is *forced* to reply: "Pleased to meet you, Mr. Dodge." If he didn't, he would have the terrible hounds of democracy on his heels and at his throat, the moment he landed in the Land of the Free. An Englishman is free to continue unaware of the existence of a fellow-countryman, if the looks of that fellow-countryman are distasteful. But every American citizen is free to force his presence upon you, no matter how unwilling you may be.

Freedom!

The Effinghams detest Mr. Dodge. They abhor him. They loathe and despise him. They have an unmitigated contempt for him. Everything he is, says, and does, seems to them too vulgar, too despicable. Yet they are forced to answer, when he presents himself: "Pleased to meet you, Mr. Dodge."

Freedom!

Mr. Dodge, of Dodge-town, alternately fawns and intrudes, cringes and bullies. And the Effinghams, terribly "superior" in a land of equality, writhe helpless. They would fain snub Septimus out of existence. But Septimus is not to be snubbed. As a true democrat, he is unsnubbable. As a true democrat, he has right on his side. And right is might.

Right is might. It is the old struggle for power.

Septimus, as a true democrat, is the equal of any man. As a true democrat with a full pocket, he is, by the amount that fills his pocket, so much the superior of the democrats with empty pockets. Because, though all men are born equal and die equal, you will not get anybody to admit that ten dollars equal ten thousand dollars. No, no, there's a difference there, however far you may push equality.

Septimus has the Effinghams on the hip. He has them fast, and they will not escape. What tortures await them at home, in the Land of the Free, at the hands of the hideously affable Dodge, we do not care to disclose. What was the persecution of a haughty Lord or a marauding Baron or an inquisitorial Abbot compared to the persecution of a million Dodges? The proud Effinghams are like men buried naked to the chin in ant-heaps, to be bitten into extinction by a myriad ants. Stoically, as good democrats and idealists, they writhe and endure, without making too much moan.

They writhe and endure. There is no escape. Not from that time to this. No escape. They writhed on the horns of the Dodge dilemma.

Since then Ford has gone one worse.

Through these white novels of Cooper runs this acid of ant-bites, the formic acid of democratic poisoning. The Effinghams feel superior. Cooper felt superior. Mrs. Cooper felt superior too. And bitten.

For they were democrats. They didn't believe in kings, or lords, or masters, or real superiority of any sort. Before God, of course. In the sight of God, of course, all men were equal. This they believed. And therefore, though they *felt* terribly superior to Mr. Dodge, yet, since they were his equals in the sight of God, they could not feel free to say to him: "Mr. Dodge, please go to the devil." They had to say: "Pleased to meet you."

What a lie to tell! Democratic lies.

What a dilemma! To feel so superior. To *know* you are superior. And yet to believe that, in the sight of God, you are equal. Can't help yourself.

Why couldn't they let the Lord Almighty look after the equality, since it seems to happen specifically in His sight, and stick themselves to their own superiority. Why couldn't they?

Somehow they daren't.

They were Americans, idealists. How dare they balance a mere intense feeling against an IDEA and an IDEAL?

Ideally—i.e., in the sight of God, Mr. Dodge was their equal.

What a low opinion they held of the Almighty's faculty for discrimination.

But it was so. The IDEAL of EQUALITY.

Pleased to meet you, Mr. Dodge.

We are equal in the sight of God, of course. But er——

Very glad to meet you, Miss Effingham. Did you say—
er? Well now, I think my bank balance will bear it.

Poor Eve Effingham.

Eve! Think of it. Eve! And birds of paradise. And
apples.

And Mr. Dodge.

This is where apples of knowledge get you, Miss Eve.
You should leave 'em alone.

"Mr. Dodge, you are a hopeless and insufferable inferior."

Why couldn't she say it? She felt it. And she was a
heroine.

Alas, she was an American heroine. She was an EDUCATED
WOMAN. She KNEW all about IDEALS. She swallowed the
IDEAL of EQUALITY with her first mouthful of KNOWLEDGE.
Alas for her and that apple of Sodom that looked so rosy.
Alas for all her knowing.

Mr. Dodge (in check knickerbockers): Well, feeling a
little uncomfortable below the belt, are you, Miss
Effingham?

Miss Effingham (with difficulty withdrawing her gaze
from the INFINITE OCEAN): Good morning, Mr. Dodge. I
was admiring the dark blue distance.

Mr. Dodge: Say, couldn't you admire something a bit
nearer?

Think how easy it would have been for her to say "Go
away!" or "Leave me, varlet!"—or "Hence, base-born
knave!" Or just to turn her back on him.

But then he would simply have marched round to the
other side of her.

Was she his superior, or wasn't she?

Why surely, intrinsically, she *was.* Intrinsically Fenimore
Cooper was the superior of the Dodges of his day. He felt
it. But he felt he ought not to feel it. And he never had it
out with himself.

That is why one rather gets impatient with him. He feels
he is superior, and feels he ought *not* to feel so, and is
therefore rather snobbish, and at the same time a little
apologetic. Which is surely tiresome.

If a man feels superior, he should have it out with himself. "Do I feel superior because I *am* superior? Or is it
just the snobbishness of class, or education, or money?"

Class, education, money won't make a man superior. But

if he's just *born* superior, in himself, there it is. Why deny it?

It is a nasty sight to see the Effinghams putting themselves at the mercy of a Dodge, just because of a mere idea or ideal. Fools. They ruin more than they know. Because at the same time they are snobbish.

Septimus at the Court of King Arthur.

Septimus: Hello, Arthur! Pleased to meet you. By the way, what's all that great long sword about?

Arthur: This is Excalibur, the sword of my knighthood and my kingship.

Septimus: That so! We're all equal in the sight of God, you know, Arthur.

Arthur: Yes.

Septimus: Then I guess it's about time I had that yard-and-a-half of Excalibur to play with. Don't you think so? We're equal in the sight of God, and you've had it for quite a while.

Arthur: Yes, I agree. (Hands him Excalibur.)

Septimus (prodding Arthur with Excalibur): Say, Art, which is your fifth rib?

Superiority is a sword. Hand it over to Septimus, and you'll get it back between your ribs.—The whole moral of democracy.

But there you are. Eve Effingham had pinned herself down on the *Contrat Social*, and she was prouder of that pin through her body than of any mortal thing else. Her IDEAL. Her IDEAL of DEMOCRACY.

When America set out to destroy Kings and Lords and Masters, and the whole paraphernalia of European superiority, it pushed a pin right through its own body, and on that pin it still flaps and buzzes and twists in misery. The pin of democratic equality. Freedom.

There'll never be any life in America till you pull the pin out and admit natural inequality. Natural superiority, natural inferiority. Till such time, Americans just buzz round like various sorts of propellers, pinned down by their freedom and equality.

That's why these white novels of Fenimore Cooper are only historically and sardonically interesting. The people are all pinned down by some social pin, and buzzing away in social importance or friction, round and round on the pin. Never real human beings. Always things pinned down, choosing to be pinned down, transfixed by the idea or ideal of equality and democracy, on which they turn loudly and importantly, like propellers propelling. These States. Humanly, it is boring. As a historic phenomenon, it is amazing, ludicrous, and irritating.

If you don't pull the pin out in time, you'll never be able to pull it out. You must turn on it for ever, or bleed to death.

> "Naked to the waist was I,
> And deep within my breast did lie,
> Though no man any blood could spy,
> The truncheon of a spear——"

Is it already too late?

Oh God, the democratic pin!

Freedom, Equality, Equal Opportunity, Education, Rights of Man.

The pin! The pin!

Well, there buzzes Eve Effingham, snobbishly impaled. She is a perfect American heroine, and I'm sure she wore the first smartly-tailored "suit" that ever woman wore. I'm sure she spoke several languages. I'm sure she was hopelessly competent. I'm sure she "adored" her husband, and spent masses of his money, and divorced him because he didn't understand LOVE.

American women in their perfect "suits". American men in their imperfect coats and skirts!

I feel I'm the superior of most men I meet. Not in birth, because I never had a great-grandfather. Not in money, because I've got none. Not in education, because I'm merely scrappy. And certainly not in beauty or in manly strength.

Well, what then?

Just in myself.

When I'm challenged, I do feel myself superior to most of the men I meet. Just a natural superiority.

But not till there enters an element of challenge.

When I meet another man, and he is just himself—even if he is an ignorant Mexican pitted with small-pox—then there is no question between us of superiority or inferiority.

He is a man and I am a man. We are ourselves. There is no question between us.

But let a question arise, let there be a challenge, and then I feel he should do reverence to the gods in me, because they are more than the gods in him. And he should give reverence to the very me, because it is more at one with the gods than is his very self.

If this is conceit, I am sorry. But it's the gods in me that matter. And in other men.

As for me, I am so glad to salute the brave, reckless gods in another man. So glad to meet a man who will abide by his very self.

Ideas! Ideals! All this paper between us. What a weariness.

If only people would meet in their very selves, without wanting to put some idea over one another, or some ideal.

Damn all ideas and all ideals. Damn all the false stress, and the pins.

I am I. Here am I. Where are you?

Ah, there you are! Now, damn the consequences, we have met.

That's my idea of democracy, if you can call it an idea.

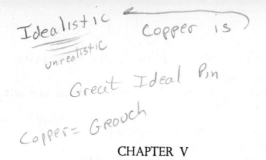

CHAPTER V

FENIMORE COOPER'S LEATHERSTOCKING NOVELS

IN his Leatherstocking books, Fenimore is off on another track. He is no longer concerned with social white Americans that buzz with pins through them, buzz loudly against every mortal thing except the pin itself. The pin of the Great Ideal.

One gets irritated with Cooper because he never for once snarls at the Great Ideal Pin which transfixes him. No, indeed. Rather he tries to push it through the very heart of the Continent.

But I have loved the Leatherstocking books so dearly. Wish-fulfilment!

Anyhow, one is not supposed to take LOVE seriously, in these books. Eve Effingham, impaled on the social pin, conscious all the time of her own ego and of nothing else, suddenly fluttering in throes of love: no, it makes me sick. LOVE is never LOVE until it has a pin pushed through it and becomes an IDEAL. The ego, turning on a pin, is wildly IN LOVE, always. Because that's the thing to be.

Cooper was a GENTLEMAN, in the worst sense of the word. In the Nineteenth Century sense of the word. A correct, clock-work man.

Not altogether, of course.

The great national Grouch was grinding inside him. Probably he called it COSMIC URGE. Americans usually do: in capital letters.

Best stick to National Grouch. The great American grouch.

Cooper had it, gentleman that he was. That is why he flitted round Europe so uneasily. Of course, in Europe he could be, and was, a gentleman to his heart's content.

"In short," he says in one of his letters, "we were at table two counts, one monsignore, an English Lord, an Ambassador, and my humble self."

47

Were we really!

How nice it must have been to know that one self, at least, was humble.

And he felt the democratic American tomahawk wheeling over his uncomfortable scalp all the time.

The great American grouch.

Two monsters loomed on Cooper's horizon.

MRS. COOPER	MY WORK
MY WORK	MY WIFE
MY WIFE	MY WORK

THE DEAR CHILDREN
MY WORK!!!

There you have the essential keyboard of Cooper's soul.

If there is one thing that annoys me more than a business man and his BUSINESS, it is an artist, a writer, painter, musician, and MY WORK. When an artist says MY WORK, the flesh goes tired on my bones. When he says MY WIFE, I want to hit him.

Cooper grizzled about his work. Oh, heaven, he cared so much whether it was good or bad, and what the French thought, and what Mr. Snippy Knowall said, and how Mrs. Cooper took it. The pin, the pin!

But he was truly an artist: then an American: then a gentleman.

And the grouch grouched inside him, through all.

They seem to have been specially fertile in imagining themselves "under the wigwam", do these Americans, just when their knees were comfortably under the mahogany, in Paris, along with the knees of

4 Counts
2 Cardinals
1 Milord
5 Cocottes
1 Humble self

You bet, though, that when the cocottes were being raffled off, Fenimore went home to his WIFE.

Wish Fulfilment		Actuality
THE WIGWAM	vs.	MY HOTEL
CHINGACHGOOK	vs.	MY WIFE
NATTY BUMPPO	vs.	MY HUMBLE SELF

Fenimore, lying in his Louis Quatorze hotel in Paris, passionately musing about Natty Bumppo and the pathless forest, and mixing his imagination with the Cupids and Butterflies on the painted ceiling, while Mrs. Cooper was struggling with her latest gown in the next room, and the déjeuner was with the Countess at eleven. . . .

Men live by lies.

In actuality, Fenimore loved the genteel continent of Europe, and waited gasping for the newspapers to praise his WORK.

In another actuality he loved the tomahawking continent of America, and imagined himself Natty Bumppo.

His actual desire was to be: *Monsieur Fenimore Cooper, le grand écrivain américain.*

His innermost wish was to be: Natty Bumppo.

Now Natty and Fenimore, arm-in-arm, are an odd couple.

You can see Fenimore: blue coat, silver buttons, silver-and-diamond buckle shoes, ruffles.

You see Natty Bumppo: a grizzled, uncouth old renegade, with gaps in his old teeth and a drop on the end of his nose.

But Natty was Fenimore's great wish: his wish-fulfilment.

"It was a matter of course," says Mrs. Cooper, "that he should dwell on the better traits of the picture rather than on the coarser and more revolting, though more common points. Like West, he could see Apollo in the young Mohawk."

The coarser and more revolting, though more common points.

You see now why he depended so absolutely on MY WIFE. She had to look things in the face for him. The coarser and more revolting, and certainly more common points, she had to see.

He himself did so love seeing pretty-pretty, with the thrill of a red scalp now and then.

Fenimore, in his imagination, wanted to be Natty Bumppo, who, I am sure, belched after he had eaten his dinner. At the same time Mr. Cooper was nothing if not a gentleman. So he decided to stay in France and have it all his own way.

In France, Natty would not belch after eating, and Chingachgook could be all the Apollo he liked.

As if ever any Indian was like Apollo. The Indians, with their curious female quality, their archaic figures, with high shoulders and deep, archaic waists, like a sort of woman! And their natural devilishness, their natural insidiousness.

But men see what they want to see: especially if they look from a long distance, across the ocean, for example.

Yet the Leatherstocking books are lovely. Lovely half-lies. They form a sort of American Odyssey, with Natty Bumppo for Odysseus.

Only, in the original Odyssey, there is plenty of devil, Circes and swine and all. And Ithacus is devil enough to outwit the devils. But Natty is a saint with a gun, and the Indians are gentlemen through and through, though they may take an occasional scalp.

There are five Leatherstocking novels: a *decrescendo* of reality, and a crescendo of beauty.

1. *Pioneers:* A raw frontier-village on Lake Champlain, at the end of the eighteenth century. Must be a picture of Cooper's home, as he knew it when a boy. A very lovely book. Natty Bumppo an old man, an old hunter half civilized.

2. *The Last of the Mohicans:* A historical fight between the British and the French, with Indians on both sides, at a Fort by Lake Champlain. Romantic flight of the British general's two daughters, conducted by the scout, Natty, who is in the prime of life; romantic death of the last of the Delawares.

3. *The Prairie:* A wagon of some huge, sinister Kentuckians trekking west into the unbroken prairie. Prairie Indians, and Natty, an old, old man; he dies seated on a chair on the Rocky Mountains, looking east.

4. *The Pathfinder:* The Great Lakes. Natty, a man of about thirty-five, makes an abortive proposal to a bouncing damsel, daughter of the Sergeant at the Fort.

5. *Deerslayer:* Natty and Hurry Harry, both quite young, are hunting in the virgin wild. They meet two white women. Lake Champlain again.

These are the five Leatherstocking books: Natty Bumppo

being Leatherstocking, Pathfinder, Deerslayer, according to his ages.

Now let me put aside my impatience at the unreality of this vision, and accept it as a wish-fulfilment vision, a kind of yearning myth. Because it seems to me that the things in Cooper that make one so savage, when one compares them with actuality, are perhaps, when one considers them as presentations of a deep subjective desire, real in their way, and almost prophetic.

The passionate love for America, for the soil of America, for example. As I say, it is perhaps easier to love America passionately, when you look at it through the wrong end of the telescope, across all the Atlantic water, as Cooper did so often, than when you are right there. When you are actually *in* America, America hurts, because it has a powerful disintegrative influence upon the white psyche. It is full of grinning, unappeased aboriginal demons, too, ghosts, and it persecutes the white men, like some Eumenides, until the white men give up their absolute whiteness. America is tense with latent violence and resistance. The very common sense of white Americans has a tinge of helplessness in it, and deep fear of what might be if they were not common-sensical.

Yet one day the demons of America must be placated, the ghosts must be appeased, the Spirit of Place atoned for. Then the true passionate love for American Soil will appear. As yet, there is too much menace in the landscape.

But probably, one day America will be as beautiful in actuality as it is in Cooper. Not yet, however. When the factories have fallen down again.

And again, this perpetual blood-brother theme of the Leatherstocking novels, Natty and Chingachgook, the Great Serpent. At present it is a sheer myth. The Red Man and the White Man are not blood-brothers: even when they are most friendly. When they are most friendly, it is as a rule the one betraying his race-spirit to the other. In the white man—rather high-brow—who "loves" the Indian, one feels the white man betraying his own race. There is something unproud, underhand in it. Renegade. The same with the Americanised Indian who believes absolutely in the white mode. It is a betrayal. Renegade again.

In the actual flesh, it seems to me the white man and the

red man cause a feeling of oppression, the one to the other, no matter what the good will. The red life flows in a different direction from the white life. You can't make two streams that flow in opposite directions meet and mingle soothingly.

Certainly, if Cooper had had to spend his whole life in the backwoods, side by side with a Noble Red Brother, he would have screamed with the oppression of suffocation. He had to have Mrs. Cooper, a straight strong pillar of society, to hang on to. And he had to have the culture of France to turn back to, or he would just have been stifled. The Noble Red Brother would have smothered him and driven him mad.

So that the Natty and Chingachgook myth must remain a myth. It is a wish-fulfilment, an evasion of actuality. As we have said before, the folds of the Great Serpent would have been heavy, very heavy, too heavy, on any white man. Unless the white man were a true renegade, hating himself and his own race-spirit, as sometimes happens.

It seems there can be no fusion in the flesh. But the spirit can change. The white man's spirit can never become as the red man's spirit. It doesn't want to. But it can cease to be the opposite and the negative of the red man's spirit. It can open out a new great area of consciousness, in which there is room for the red spirit too.

To open out a new wide area of consciousness means to slough the old consciousness. The old consciousness has become a tight-fitting prison to us, in which we are going rotten.

You can't have a new, easy skin before you have sloughed the old, tight skin.

You can't.

And you just can't, so you may as well leave off pretending.

Now the essential history of the people of the United States seems to me just this: At the Renaissance the old consciousness was becoming a little tight. Europe sloughed her last skin, and started a new, final phase.

But some Europeans recoiled from the last final phase. They wouldn't enter the *cul de sac* of post-Renaissance, "liberal" Europe. They came to America.

They came to America for two reasons:

1. To slough the old European consciousness completely.
2. To grow a new skin underneath, a new form. This second is a hidden process.

The two processes go on, of course, simultaneously. The slow forming of the new skin underneath is the slow sloughing of the old skin. And sometimes this immortal serpent feels very happy, feeling a new golden glow of a strangely-patterned skin envelop him: and sometimes he feels very sick, as if his very entrails were being torn out of him, as he wrenches once more at his old skin, to get out of it.

Out! Out! he cries, in all kinds of euphemisms.

He's got to have his new skin on him before ever he can get out.

And he's got to get out before his new skin can ever be his own skin.

So there he is, a torn, divided monster.

The true American, who writhes and writhes like a snake that is long in sloughing.

Sometimes snakes can't slough. They can't burst their old skin. Then they go sick and die inside the old skin, and nobody ever sees the new pattern.

It needs a real desperate recklessness to burst your old skin at last. You simply don't care what happens to you, if you rip yourself in two, so long as you do get out.

It also needs a real belief in the new skin. Otherwise you are likely never to make the effort. Then you gradually sicken and go rotten and die in the old skin.

Now Fenimore stayed very safe inside the old skin: a gentleman, almost a European, as proper as proper can be. And, safe inside the old skin, he *imagined* the gorgeous American pattern of a new skin.

He hated democracy. So he evaded it, and had a nice dream of something beyond democracy. But he belonged to democracy all the while.

Evasion!—Yet even that doesn't make the dream worthless.

Democracy in America was never the same as Liberty in Europe. In Europe Liberty was a great life-throb. But in America Democracy was always something anti-life. The greatest democrats, like Abraham Lincoln, had always a sacrificial, self-murdering note in their voices. American Democracy was a form of self-murder, always. Or of murdering somebody else.

Necessarily. It was a *pis aller*. It was the *pis aller* to European Liberty. It was a cruel form of sloughing. Men murdered themselves into this democracy. Democracy is the utter hardening of the old skin, the old form, the old psyche. It hardens till it is tight and fixed and inorganic. Then it *must* burst, like a chrysalis shell. And out must come the soft grub, or the soft damp butterfly of the American-at-last.

America has gone the *pis aller* of her democracy. Now she must slough even that, chiefly that, indeed.

What did Cooper dream beyond democracy? Why, in his immortal friendship of Chingachgook and Natty Bumppo he dreamed the nucleus of a new society. That is, he dreamed a new human relationship. A stark, stripped human relationship of two men, deeper than the deeps of sex. Deeper than property, deeper than fatherhood, deeper than marriage, deeper than love. So deep that it is loveless. The stark, loveless, wordless unison of two men who have come to the bottom of themselves. This is the new nucleus of a new society, the clue to a new world-epoch. It asks for a great and cruel sloughing first of all. Then it finds a great release into a new world, a new moral, a new landscape.

Natty and the Great Serpent are neither equals nor unequals. Each obeys the other when the moment arrives. And each is stark and dumb in the other's presence, starkly himself, without illusion created. Each is just the crude pillar of a man, the crude living column of his own manhood. And each knows the godhead of this crude column of manhood. A new relationship.

The Leatherstocking novels create the myth of this new relation. And they go backwards, from old age to golden youth. That is the true myth of America. She starts old, old, wrinkled and writhing in an old skin. And there is a gradual sloughing of the old skin, towards a new youth. It is the myth of America.

You start with actuality. *Pioneers* is no doubt Cooperstown, when Cooperstown was in the stage of inception: a village of one wild street of log cabins under the forest hills by Lake Champlain: a village of crude, wild frontiersmen, reacting against civilization.

Towards this frontier-village in the winter time, a negro slave drives a sledge through the mountains, over deep snow. In the sledge sits a fair damsel, Miss Temple, with her handsome pioneer father, Judge Temple. They hear a shot in the trees. It is the old hunter and backwoodsman, Natty Bumppo, long and lean and uncouth, with a long rifle and gaps in his teeth.

Judge Temple is "squire" of the village, and he has a ridiculous, commodious "hall" for his residence. It is still the old English form. Miss Temple is a pattern young lady, like Eve Effingham: in fact, she gets a young and very genteel but impoverished Effingham for a husband. The old world holding its own on the edge of the wild. A bit tiresomely too, with rather more prunes and prisms than one can digest. Too romantic.

Against the "hall" and the gentry, the real frontiers-folk, the rebels. The two groups meet at the village inn, and at the frozen church, and at the Christmas sports, and on the ice of the lake, and at the great pigeon shoot. It is a beautiful, resplendent picture of life. Fenimore puts in only the glamour.

Perhaps my taste is childish, but these scenes in *Pioneers* seem to me marvellously beautiful. The raw village street, with woodfires blinking through the unglazed window-chinks, on a winter's night. The inn, with the rough woodsman and the drunken Indian John; the church, with the snowy congregation crowding to the fire. Then the lavish abundance of Christmas cheer, and turkey-shooting in the snow. Spring coming, forests all green, maple-sugar taken from the trees: and clouds of pigeons flying from the south, myriads of pigeons, shot in heaps; and night-fishing on the teeming, virgin lake; and deer-hunting.

Pictures! Some of the loveliest, most glamorous pictures in all literature.

Alas, without the cruel iron of reality. It is all real enough. Except that one realizes that Fenimore was writing from a safe distance, where he would idealize and have his wish-fulfilment.

Because, when one comes to America, one finds that there is always a certain slightly devilish resistance in the

American landscape, and a certain slightly bitter resistance in the white man's heart. Hawthorne gives this. But Cooper glosses it over.

The American landscape has never been at one with the white man. Never. And white men have probably never felt so bitter anywhere, as here in America, where the very landscape, in its very beauty, seems a bit devilish and grinning, opposed to us.

Cooper, however, glosses over this resistance, which in actuality can never quite be glossed over. He *wants* the landscape to be at one with him. So he goes away to Europe and sees it as such. It is a sort of vision.

And, nevertheless, the oneing will surely take place— some day.

The myth is the story of Natty. The old, lean hunter and backwoodsman lives with his friend, the grey-haired Indian John, an old Delaware chief, in a hut within reach of the village. The Delaware is christianized and bears the Christian name of John. He is tribeless and lost. He humiliates his grey hairs in drunkenness, and dies, thankful to be dead, in a forest fire, passing back to the fire whence he derived.

And this is Chingachgook, the splendid Great Serpent of the later novels.

No doubt Cooper, as a boy, knew both Natty and the Indian John. No doubt they fired his imagination even then. When he is a man, crystallized in society and sheltering behind the safe pillar of Mrs. Cooper, these two old fellows become a myth to his soul. He traces himself to a new youth in them.

As for the story: Judge Temple has just been instrumental in passing the wise game laws. But Natty has lived by his gun all his life in the wild woods, and simply childishly cannot understand how he can be poaching on the Judge's land among the pine trees. He shoots a deer in the close season. The Judge is all sympathy, but the law *must* be enforced. Bewildered Natty, an old man of seventy, is put in stocks and in prison. They release him as soon as possible. But the thing was done.

The letter killeth.

Natty's last connexion with his own race is broken. John, the Indian, is dead. The old hunter disappears, lonely and severed, into the forest, away, away from his race.

In the new epoch that is coming, there will be no letter of the Law.

Chronologically, *The Last of the Mohicans* follows *Pioneers*. But in the myth, *The Prairie* comes next.

Cooper of course knew his own America. He travelled west and saw the prairies, and camped with the Indians of the prairie.

The Prairie, like *Pioneers*, bears a good deal the stamp of actuality. It is a strange, splendid book, full of sense of doom. The figures of the great Kentuckian men, with their wolf-women, loom colossal on the vast prairie, as they camp with their wagons. These are different pioneers from Judge Temple. Lurid, brutal, tinged with the sinisterness of crime; these are the gaunt white men who push west, push on and on against the natural opposition of the continent. On towards a doom. Great wings of vengeful doom seem spread over the west, grim against the intruder. You feel them again in Frank Norris' novel, *The Octopus*. While in the West of Bret Harte there is a very devil in the air, and beneath him are sentimental self-conscious people being wicked and goody by evasion.

In *The Prairie* there is a shadow of violence and dark cruelty flickering in the air. It is the aboriginal demon hovering over the core of the continent. It hovers still, and the dread is still there.

Into such a prairie enters the huge figure of Ishmael, ponderous, pariah-like Ishmael and his huge sons and his were-wolf wife. With their wagons they roll on from the frontiers of Kentucky, like Cyclops into the savage wilderness. Day after day they seem to force their way into oblivion. But their force of penetration ebbs. They are brought to a stop. They recoil in the throes of murder and entrench themselves in isolation on a hillock in the midst of the prairie. There they hold out like demi-gods against the elements and the subtle Indian.

The pioneering brute invasion of the West, crime-tinged!

And into this setting, as a sort of minister of peace, enters the old, old hunter Natty, and his suave, horse-riding Sioux Indians. But he seems like a shadow.

The hills rise softly west, to the Rockies. There seems a

new peace: or is it only suspense, abstraction, waiting? Is it only a sort of beyond?

Natty lives in these hills, in a village of the suave, horse-riding Sioux. They revere him as an old wise father.

In these hills he dies, sitting in his chair and looking far east, to the forest and great sweet waters, whence he came. He dies gently, in physical peace with the land and the Indians. He is an old, old man.

Cooper could see no further than the foothills where Natty died, beyond the prairie.

The other novels bring us back east.

The Last of the Mohicans is divided between real historical narrative and true "romance". For myself, I prefer the romance. It has a myth meaning, whereas the narrative is chiefly record.

For the first time we get actual women: the dark, handsome Cora and her frail sister, the White Lily. The good old division, the dark sensual woman and the clinging, submissive little blonde, who is so "pure"

These sisters are fugitives through the forest, under the protection of a Major Heyward, a young American officer and Englishman. He is just a "white" man, very good and brave and generous, etc., but limited, most definitely *borné*. He would probably love Cora, if he dared, but he finds it safer to adore the clinging White Lily of a younger sister.

This trio is escorted by Natty, now Leatherstocking, a hunter and scout in the prime of life, accompanied by his inseparable friend Chingachgook, and the Delaware's beautiful son—Adonis rather than Apollo—Uncas, The last of the Mohicans.

There is also a "wicked" Indian, Magua, handsome and injured incarnation of evil.

Cora is the scarlet flower of womanhood, fierce, passionate offspring of some mysterious union between the British officer and a Creole woman in the West Indies. Cora loves Uncas, Uncas loves Cora. But Magua also desires Cora, violently desires her. A lurid little circle of sensual fire. So Fenimore kills them all off, Cora, Uncas, and Magua, and leaves the White Lily to carry on the race. She will breed plenty of white children to Major Heyward. These tiresome "lilies that fester", of our day.

Evidently Cooper—or the artist in him—has decided that

there can be no blood-mixing of the two races, white and red. He kills 'em off.

Beyond all this heart-beating stand the figures of Natty and Chingachgook: the two childless, womanless men, of opposite races. They are the abiding thing. Each of them is alone, and final in his race. And they stand side by side, stark, abstract, beyond emotion, yet eternally together. All the other loves seem frivolous. This is the new great thing, the clue, the inception of a new humanity.

And Natty, what sort of a white man is he? Why, he is a man with a gun. He is a killer, a slayer. Patient and gentle as he is, he is a slayer. Self-effacing, self-forgetting, still he is a killer.

Twice, in the book, he brings an enemy down hurtling in death through the air, downwards. Once it is the beautiful, wicked Magua—shot from a height, and hurtling down ghastly through space, into death.

This is Natty, the white forerunner. A killer. As in *Deerslayer*, he shoots the bird that flies in the high, high sky, so that the bird falls out of the invisible into the visible, dead, he symbolizes himself. He will bring the bird of the spirit out of the high air. He is the stoic American killer of the old great life. But he kills, as he says, only to live.

Pathfinder takes us to the Great Lakes, and the glamour and beauty of sailing the great sweet waters. Natty is now called Pathfinder. He is about thirty-five years old, and he falls in love. The damsel is Mabel Dunham, daughter of Sergeant Dunham of the Fort garrison. She is blonde and in all things admirable. No doubt Mrs. Cooper was very much like Mabel.

And Pathfinder doesn't marry her. She won't have him. She wisely prefers a more comfortable Jasper. So Natty goes off to grouch, and to end by thanking his stars. When he had got right clear, and sat by the campfire with Chingachgook, in the forest, didn't he just thank his stars! A lucky escape!

Men of an uncertain age are liable to these infatuations. They aren't always lucky enough to be rejected.

Whatever would poor Mabel have done, had she been Mrs. Bumppo?

Natty had no business marrying. His mission was elsewhere.

The most fascinating Leatherstocking book is the last, *Deerslayer*. Natty is now a fresh youth, called Deerslayer. But the kind of silent prim youth who is never quite young, but reserves himself for different things.

It is a gem of a book. Or a bit of perfect paste. And myself, I like a bit of perfect paste in a perfect setting, so long as I am not fooled by pretence of reality. And the setting of Deerslayer *could* not be more exquisite. Lake Champlain again.

Of course it never rains: it is never cold and muddy and dreary: no one has wet feet or toothache: no one ever feels filthy, when they can't wash for a week. God knows what the women would really have looked like, for they fled through the wilds without soap, comb, or towel. They breakfasted off a chunk of meat, or nothing, lunched the same, and supped the same.

Yet at every moment they are elegant, perfect ladies, in correct toilet.

Which isn't quite fair. You need only go camping for a week, and you'll see.

But it is a myth, not a realistic tale. Read it as a lovely myth. Lake Glimmerglass.

Deerslayer, the youth with the long rifle, is found in the woods with a big, handsome, blonde-bearded backwoodsman called Hurry Harry. Deerslayer seems to have been born under a hemlock tree out of a pine-cone: a young man of the woods. He is silent, simple, philosophic, moralistic, and an unerring shot. His simplicity is the simplicity of age rather than of youth. He is race-old. All his reactions and impulses are fixed, static. Almost he is sexless, so race-old. Yet intelligent, hardy, dauntless.

Hurry Harry is a big blusterer, just the opposite of Deerslayer. Deerslayer keeps the centre of his own consciousness steady and unperturbed. Hurry Harry is one of those floundering people who bluster from one emotion to another, very self-conscious, without any centre to them.

These two young men are making their way to a lovely, smallish lake, Lake Glimmerglass. On this water the Hutter family has established itself. Old Hutter, it is suggested, has a criminal, coarse, buccaneering past, and is a sort of fugitive from justice. But he is a good enough father to his two grown-up girls. The family lives in a log hut "castle", built on piles in the water, and the old man has also con-structed an "ark", a sort of house-boat, in which he can take his daughters when he goes on his rounds to trap the beaver.

The two girls are the inevitable dark and light. Judith, dark, fearless, passionate, a little lurid with sin, is the scarlet-and-black blossom. Hetty, the younger, blonde, frail and innocent, is the white lily again. But alas, the lily has begun to fester. She is slightly imbecile.

The two hunters arrive at the lake among the woods just as war has been declared. The Hutters are unaware of the fact. And hostile Indians are on the lake already. So, the story of thrills and perils.

Thomas Hardy's inevitable division of women into dark and fair, sinful and innocent, sensual and pure, is Cooper's division too. It is indicative of the desire in the man. He wants sensuality and sin, and he wants purity and "inno-cence". If the innocence goes a little rotten, slightly im-becile, bad luck!

Hurry Harry, of course, like a handsome impetuous meat-fly, at once wants Judith, the lurid poppy-blossom. Judith rejects him with scorn.

Judith, the sensual woman, at once wants the quiet, reserved, unmastered Deerslayer. She wants to master him. And Deerslayer is half tempted, but never more than half. He is not going to be mastered. A philosophic old soul, he does not give much for the temptations of sex. Probably he dies virgin.

And he is right of it. Rather than be dragged into a false heat of deliberate sensuality, he will remain alone. His soul is alone, for ever alone. So he will preserve his integrity, and remain alone in the flesh. It is a stoicism which is honest and fearless, and from which Deerslayer never lapses, except when, approaching middle age, he proposes to the buxom Mabel.

He lets his consciousness penetrate in loneliness into the new continent. His contacts are not human. He wrestles with the spirits of the forest and the American wild, as a hermit wrestles with God and Satan. His one meeting is with Chingachgook, and this meeting is silent, reserved, across an unpassable distance.

Hetty, the White Lily, being imbecile, although full of

vaporous religion and the dear, good God, "who governs all things by his providence", is hopelessly infatuated with Hurry Harry. Being innocence gone imbecile, like Dostoevsky's Idiot, she longs to give herself to the handsome meat-fly. Of course he doesn't want her.

And so nothing happens: in that direction. Deerslayer goes off to meet Chingachgook, and help him woo an Indian maid. Vicarious.

It is the miserable story of the collapse of the white psyche. The white man's mind and soul are divided between these two things: innocence and lust, the Spirit and Sensuality. Sensuality always carries a stigma, and is therefore more deeply desired, or lusted after. But spirituality alone gives the sense of uplift, exaltation, and "winged life", with the inevitable reaction into sin and spite. So the white man is divided against himself. He plays off one side of himself against the other side, till it is really a tale told by an idiot, and nauseating.

Against this, one is forced to admire the stark, enduring figure of Deerslayer. He is neither spiritual nor sensual. He is a moralizer, but he always tries to moralize from actual experience, not from theory. He says: "Hurt nothing unless you're forced to." Yet he gets his deepest thrill of gratification, perhaps, when he puts a bullet through the heart of a beautiful buck, as it stoops to drink at the lake. Or when he brings the invisible bird fluttering down in death, out of the high blue. "Hurt nothing unless you're forced to." And yet he lives by death, by killing the wild things of the air and earth.

It's not good enough.

But you have there the myth of the essential white America. All the other stuff, the love, the democracy, the floundering into lust, is a sort of by-play. The essential American soul is hard, isolate, stoic, and a killer. It has never yet melted.

Of course, the soul often breaks down into disintegration, and you have lurid sin and Judith, imbecile innocence lusting, in Hetty, and bluster, bragging, and self-conscious strength, in Harry. But there are the disintegration products.

What true myth concerns itself with is not the disintegration product. True myth concerns itself centrally with the onward adventure of the integral soul. And this, for America, is Deerslayer. A man who turns his back on white society. A man who keeps his moral integrity hard and intact. An isolate, almost selfless, stoic, enduring man, who lives by death, by killing, but who is pure white.

This is the very intrinsic-most American. He is at the core of all the other flux and fluff. And when *this* man breaks from his static isolation, and makes a new move, then look out, something will be happening.

CHAPTER VI

EDGAR ALLAN POE

POE has no truck with Indians or Nature. He makes no bones about Red Brothers and Wigwams.

He is absolutely concerned with the disintegration-processes of his own psyche. As we have said, the rhythm of American art-activity is dual.

1. A disintegrating and sloughing of the old consciousness.

2. The forming of a new consciousness underneath.

Fenimore Cooper has the two vibrations going on together. Poe has only one, only the disintegrative vibration. This makes him almost more a scientist than an artist.

Moralists have always wondered helplessly why Poe's "morbid" tales need have been written. They need to be written because old things need to die and disintegrate, because the old white psyche has to be gradually broken down before anything else can come to pass.

Man must be stripped even of himself. And it is a painful, sometimes a ghastly process.

Poe had a pretty bitter doom. Doomed to seethe down his soul in a great continuous convulsion of disintegration, and doomed to register the process. And then doomed to be abused for it, when he had performed some of the bitterest tasks of human experience, that can be asked of a man. Necessary tasks, too. For the human soul must suffer its own disintegration, *consciously*, if ever it is to survive.

But Poe is rather a scientist than an artist. He is reducing his own self as a scientist reduces a salt in a crucible. It is an almost chemical analysis of the soul and consciousness. Whereas in true art there is always the double rhythm of creating and destroying.

This is why Poe calls his things "tales". They are a concatenation of cause and effect.

His best pieces, however, are not tales. They are more.

65

They are ghastly stories of the human soul in its disruptive throes.

Moreover, they are "love" stories.

Ligeia and *The Fall of the House of Usher* are really love stories.

Love is the mysterious vital attraction which draws things together, closer, closer together. For this reason sex is the actual crisis of love. For in sex the two blood-systems, in the male and female, concentrate and come into contact, the merest film intervening. Yet if the intervening film breaks down, it is death.

So there you are. There is a limit to everything. There is a limit to love.

The central law of all organic life is that each organism is intrinsically isolate and single in itself.

The moment its isolation breaks down, and there comes an actual mixing and confusion, death sets in.

This is true of every individual organism, from man to amœba.

But the secondary law of all organic life is that each organism only lives through contact with other matter, assimilation, and contact with other life, which means assimilation of new vibrations, non-material. Each individual organism is vivified by intimate contact with fellow organisms: up to a certain point.

So man. He breathes the air into him, he swallows food and water. But more than this. He takes into him the life of his fellow men, with whom he comes into contact, and he gives back life to them. This contact draws nearer and nearer, as the intimacy increases. When it is a whole contact, we call it love. Men live by food, but die if they eat too much. Men live by love, but die, or cause death, if they love too much.

There are two loves: sacred and profane, spiritual and sensual.

In sensual love, it is the two blood-systems, the man's and the woman's, which sweep up into pure contact, and *almost* fuse. Almost mingle. Never quite. There is always the finest imaginable wall between the two blood-waves, through which pass unknown vibrations, forces, but through which the blood itself must never break, or it means bleeding.

In spiritual love, the contact is purely nervous. The nerves in the lovers are set vibrating in unison like two instruments. The pitch can rise higher and higher. But carry this too far, and the nerves begin to break, to bleed, as it were, and a form of death sets in.

The trouble about man is that he insists on being master of his own fate, and he insists on *oneness*. For instance, having discovered the ecstasy of spiritual love, he insists that he shall have this all the time, and nothing but this, for this is life. It is what he calls "heightening" life. He wants his nerves to be set vibrating in the intense and exhilarating unison with the nerves of another being, and by this means he acquires an ecstasy of vision, he finds himself in glowing unison with all the universe.

But as a matter of fact this glowing unison is only a temporary thing, because the first law of life is that each organism is isolate in itself, it must return to its own isolation.

Yet man has tried the glow of unison, called love, and he *likes* it. It gives him his highest gratification. He wants it. He wants it all the time. He wants it and he will have it. He doesn't want to return to his own isolation. Or if he must, it is only as a prowling beast returns to its lair to rest and set out again.

This brings us to Edgar Allan Poe. The clue to him lies in the motto he chose for *Ligeia*, a quotation from the mystic Joseph Glanvill: "And the will therein lieth, which dieth not. Who knoweth the mysteries of the will, with its vigour? For God is but a great will pervading all things by nature of its intentness. Man doth not yield himself to the angels, nor unto death utterly, save only through the weakness of his feeble will."

It is a profound saying: and a deadly one.

Because if God is a great will, then the universe is but an instrument.

I don't know what God is. But He is not simply a will. That is too simple. Too anthropomorphic. Because a man wants his own will, and nothing but his will, he needn't say that God is the same will, magnified *ad infinitum*.

For me, there may be one God, but He is nameless and unknowable.

For me, there are also many gods, that come into me

and leave me again. And they have very various wills, I must say.

But the point is Poe.

Poe had experienced the ecstasies of extreme spiritual love. And he wanted those ecstasies and nothing but those ecstasies. He wanted that great gratification, the sense of flowing, the sense of unison, the sense of heightening of life. He had experienced this gratification. He was told on every hand that this ecstasy of spiritual, nervous love was the greatest thing in life, was life itself. And he had tried it for himself, he knew that for him it *was* life itself. So he wanted it. And he *would have* it. He set up his will against the whole of the limitations of nature.

This is a brave man, acting on his own belief, and his own experience. But it is also an arrogant man, and a fool.

Poe was going to get the ecstasy and the heightening, cost what it might. He went on in a frenzy, as characteristic American women nowadays go on in a frenzy, after the very same thing: the heightening, the flow, the ecstasy. Poe tried alcohol, and any drug he could lay his hand on. He also tried any human being he could lay his hands on.

His grand attempt and achievement was with his wife; his cousin, a girl with a singing voice. With her he went in for the intensest flow, the heightening, the prismatic shades of ecstasy. It was the intensest nervous vibration of unison, pressed higher and higher in pitch, till the blood-vessels of the girl broke, and the blood began to flow out loose. It was love. If you call it love.

Love can be terribly obscene.

It is love that causes the neuroticism of the day. It is love that is the prime cause of tuberculosis.

The nerves that vibrate most intensely in spiritual unisons are the sympathetic ganglia of the breast, of the throat, and the hind brain. Drive this vibration over-intensely, and you weaken the sympathetic tissues of the chest—the lungs —or of the throat, or of the lower brain, and the tubercles are given a ripe field.

But Poe drove the vibrations beyond any human pitch of endurance.

Being his cousin, she was more easily keyed to him.

Ligeia is the chief story. Ligeia! A mental-derived name.

To him the woman, his wife, was not Lucy. She was Ligeia. No doubt she even preferred it thus.

Ligeia is Poe's love-story, and its very fantasy makes it more truly his own story.

It is a tale of love pushed over a verge. And love pushed to extremes is a battle of wills between the lovers.

Love is become a battle of wills.

Which shall first destroy the other, of the lovers? Which can hold out longest, against the other?

Ligeia is still the old-fashioned woman. Her will is still to submit. She wills to submit to the vampire of her husband's consciousness. Even death.

"In stature she was tall, somewhat slender, and, in her latter days, even emaciated. I would in vain attempt to portray the majesty, the quiet ease, of her demeanour, or the incomprehensible lightness and elasticity of her footfall. . . . I was never made aware of her entrance into my closed study, save by the dear music of her low sweet voice, as she placed her marble hand upon my shoulder."

Poe has been so praised for his style. But it seems to me a meretricious affair. "Her marble hand" and "the elasticity of her footfall" seem more like chair-springs and mantel-pieces than a human creature. She never was quite a human creature to him. She was an instrument from which he got his extremes of sensation. His *machine à plaisir*, as somebody says.

All Poe's style, moreover, has this mechanical quality, as his poetry has a mechanical rhythm. He never sees anything in terms of life, almost always in terms of matter, jewels, marble, etc.,—or in terms of force, scientific. And his cadences are all managed mechanically. This is what is called "having a style".

What he wants to do with Ligeia is to analyse her, till he knows all her component parts, till he has got her all in his consciousness. She is some strange chemical salt which he must analyse out in the test-tubes of his brain, and then—when he's finished the analysis—*E finita la commedia!*

But she won't be quite analysed out. There is something, something he can't get. Writing of her eyes, he says: "They were, I must believe, far larger than the ordinary eyes of our own race"—as if anybody would want eyes "far larger" than other folks'. "They were even fuller than the fullest

of the gazelle eyes of the tribe of the valley of Nourjahad"—
which is blarney. "The hue of the orbs was the most brilliant
of black and, far over them, hung jetty lashes of great
length"—suggests a whip-lash. "The brows, slightly irregular
in outline, had the same tint. The 'strangeness', however,
which I found in the eyes, was of a nature distinct from
the formation, or the colour, or the brilliancy of the features,
and must, after all, be referred to the *expression*."—Sounds
like an anatomist anatomizing a cat—"Ah, word of no
meaning! behind whose vast latitude of mere sound we
entrench our ignorance of so much of the spiritual. The
expression of the eyes of Ligeia! How for long hours have
I pondered upon it! How have I, through the whole of a
midsummer night, struggled to fathom it! What was it—
that something more profound than the well of Democritus
—which lay far within the pupils of my beloved! What *was*
it? I was possessed with a passion to discover. . . ."

It is easy to see why each man kills the thing he loves.
To *know* a living thing is to kill it. You have to kill a
thing to know it satisfactorily. For this reason, the desirous
consciousness, the SPIRIT, is a vampire.

One should be sufficiently intelligent and interested to
know a good deal *about* any person one comes into close
contact with. *About* her. Or *about* him.

But to try to *know* any living being is to try to suck the
life out of that being.

Above all things, with the woman one loves. Every sacred
instinct teaches one that one must leave her unknown. You
know your woman darkly, in the blood. To try to *know*
her mentally is to try to kill her. Beware, oh woman, of
the man who wants to *find out what you are*. And, oh
men, beware a thousand times more of the woman who
wants to *know* you, or *get* you, what you are.

It is the temptation of a vampire fiend, is this knowledge.

Man does so horribly want to master the secret of life
and of individuality *with his mind*. It is like the analysis
of protoplasm. You can only analyse *dead* protoplasm, and
know its constituents. It is a death-process.

Keep KNOWLEDGE for the world of matter, force, and
function. It has got nothing to do with being.

But Poe wanted to know—wanted to know what was

the strangeness in the eyes of Ligeia. She might have told him it was horror at his probing, horror at being vamped by his consciousness.

But she wanted to be vamped. She wanted to be probed by his consciousness, to be KNOWN. She paid for wanting it, too.

Nowadays it is usually the man who wants to be vamped, to be KNOWN.

Edgar Allan probed and probed. So often he seemed on the verge. But she went over the verge of death before he came over the verge of knowledge. And it is always so.

He decided, therefore, that the clue to the strangeness lay in the mystery of will. "And the will therein lieth, which dieth not . . ."

Ligeia had a "gigantic volition". . . . "An intensity in thought, action, or speech was possibly, in her, a result, or at least an index" (he really meant indication) "of that gigantic volition which, during our long intercourse, failed to give other and more immediate evidence of its existence."

I should have thought her long submission to him was chief and ample "other evidence".

"Of all the women whom I have ever known, she, the outwardly calm, the ever-placid Ligeia, was the most violently a prey to the tumultuous vultures of stern passion. And of such passion I could form no estimate, save by the miraculous expansion of those eyes which at once so delighted and appalled me—by the almost magical melody, modulation, distinctness, and placidity of her very low voice—and by the fierce energy (rendered doubly effective by contrast with her manner of utterance) of the wild words which she habitually uttered."

Poor Poe, he had caught a bird of the same feather as himself. One of those terrible cravers, who crave the further sensation. Crave to madness or death. "Vultures of stern passion" indeed! Condors.

But having recognized that the clue was in her gigantic volition, he should have realized that the process of this loving, this craving, this knowing, was a struggle of wills. But Ligeia, true to the great tradition and mode of womanly love, by her will kept herself submissive, recipient. She is the passive body who is explored and analysed into death.

And yet, at times, her great female will must have revolted. "Vultures of stern passion!" With a convulsion of desire she desired his further probing and exploring. To any lengths. But then, "tumultuous vultures of stern passion". She had to fight with herself.

But Ligeia wanted to go on and on with the craving, with the love, with the sensation, with the probing, with the knowing, on and on to the end.

There is no end. There is only the rupture of death. That's where men, and women, are "had". Man is always sold, in his search for final KNOWLEDGE.

"That she loved me I should not have doubted; and I might have been easily aware that, in a bosom such as hers, love would have reigned no ordinary passion. But in death only was I fully impressed with the strength of her affection. For long hours, detaining my hand, would she pour out before me the overflowing of a heart whose more than passionate devotion amounted to idolatry." (Oh, the indecency of all this endless intimate talk!) "How had I deserved to be so blessed by such confessions?" (Another man would have felt himself cursed.) "How had I deserved to be so cursed with the removal of my beloved in the hour of her making them? But upon this subject I cannot bear to dilate. Let me say only that in Ligeia's more than womanly abandonment to a love, alas! all unmerited, all unworthily bestowed, I at length recognized the principle of her longing, with so wildly earnest a desire, for the life which was now fleeing so rapidly away. It is this wild longing—it is this eager vehemence of desire for life—*but* for life, that I have no power to portray, no utterance capable of expressing."

Well, that is ghastly enough, in all conscience.

"And from them that have not shall be taken away even that which they have."

"To him that hath life shall be given life, and from him that hath not life shall be taken away even that life which he hath."

Or her either.

These terribly conscious birds, like Poe and his Ligeia, deny the very life that is in them; they want to turn it all into talk, into *knowing*. And so life, which will *not* be known, leaves them.

But poor Ligeia, how could she help it? It was her doom. All the centuries of the SPIRIT, all the years of American rebellion against the Holy Ghost, had done it to her.

She dies, when she would rather do anything than die. And when she dies the clue, which he only lived to grasp, dies with her.

Foiled!

Foiled!

No wonder she shrieks with her last breath.

On the last day Ligeia dictates to her husband a poem. As poems go, it is rather false, meretricious. But put yourself in Ligeia's place, and it is real enough, and ghastly beyond bearing.

> "Out—out are all the lights—out all!
>   And over each quivering form
> The curtain, a funeral pall,
>   Comes down with the rush of a storm,
> While the angels, all pallid and wan,
>   Uprising, unveiling, affirm
> That the play is the tragedy, 'Man',
>   And its hero, the Conqueror Worm."

Which is the American equivalent for a William Blake poem. For Blake, too, was one of these ghastly, obscene "Knowers".

" 'O God!' half shrieked Ligeia, leaping to her feet and extending her arms aloft with a spasmodic movement, as I made an end of these lines—'O God! O Divine Father! shall these things be undeviatingly so? Shall this conqueror be not once conquered? Are we not part and parcel in Thee? Who—who knoweth the mysteries of the will with its vigour? Man doth not yield him to the angels, *nor unto death utterly*, save only through the weakness of his feeble will. ' "

So Ligeia dies. And yields to death at least partly. *Anche troppo.*

As for her cry to God—has not God said that those who sin against the Holy Ghost shall not be forgiven?

And the Holy Ghost is within us. It is the thing that prompts us to be real, not to push our own cravings too far, not to submit to stunts and high-falutin, above all, not to be too egoistic and wilful in our conscious self, but to change as the spirit inside us bids us change, and leave off when it bids us leave off, and laugh when we must laugh, particularly at ourselves, for in deadly earnestness there is always something a bit ridiculous. The Holy Ghost bids us never be too deadly in our earnestness, always to laugh in time, at ourselves and everything. Particularly at our sublimities. Everything has its hour of ridicule—everything.

Now Poe and Ligeia, alas, couldn't laugh. They were frenziedly earnest. And frenziedly they pushed on this vibration of consciousness and unison in consciousness. They sinned against the Holy Ghost that bids us all laugh and forget, bids us know our own limits. And they weren't forgiven.

Ligeia needn't blame God. She had only her own will, her "gigantic volition" to thank, lusting after more consciousness, more beastly KNOWING.

Ligeia dies. The husband goes to England, vulgarly buys or rents a gloomy, grand old abbey, puts it into some sort of repair, and furnishes it with exotic, mysterious, theatrical splendour. Never anything open and real. This theatrical "volition" of his. The bad taste of sensationalism.

Then he marries the fair-haired, blue-eyed Lady Rowena Trevanion, of Tremaine. That is, she would be a sort of Saxon-Cornish blue-blood damsel. Poor Poe!

"In halls such as these—in a bridal chamber such as this —I passed, with the Lady of Tremaine, the unhallowed hours of the first month of our marriage—passed them with but little disquietude. That my wife dreaded the fierce moodiness of my temper—that she shunned me and loved me but little—I could not help perceiving, but it gave me rather pleasure than otherwise. I loathed her with a hatred belonging more to demon than to man. My memory flew back (oh, with what intensity of regret!) to Ligeia, the beloved, the august, the beautiful, the entombed. I revelled in recollections of her purity . . ." etc.

Now the vampire lust is consciously such.

In the second month of the marriage the Lady Rowena fell ill. It is the shadow of Ligeia hangs over her. It is the ghostly Ligeia who pours poison into Rowena's cup. It is the spirit of Ligeia, leagued with the spirit of the husband, that now lusts in the slow destruction of Rowena. The two vampires, dead wife and living husband.

For Ligeia has not yielded unto death *utterly*. Her fixed, frustrated will comes back in vindictiveness. She could not have her way in life. So she, too, will find victims in life. And the husband, all the time, only uses Rowena as a living body on which to wreak his vengeance for his being thwarted with Ligeia. Thwarted from the final KNOWING her.

And at last from the corpse of Rowena, Ligeia rises. Out of her death, through the door of a corpse they have destroyed between them, reappears Ligeia, still trying to have her·will, to have more love and knowledge, the final gratification which is never final, with her husband.

For it is true, as William James and Conan Doyle and the rest allow, that a spirit can persist in the after-death. Persist by its own volition. But usually, the evil persistence of a thwarted will, returning for vengeance on life. Lemures, vampires.

It is a ghastly story of the assertion of the human will, the will-to-love and the will-to-consciousness, asserted against death itself. The pride of human conceit in KNOWLEDGE.

There are terrible spirits, ghosts, in the air of America.

Eleanora, the next story, is a fantasy revealing the sensational delights of the man in his early marriage with the young and tender bride. They dwelt, he, his cousin and her mother, in the sequestered Valley of Many-coloured Grass, the valley of prismatic sensation, where everything seems spectrum-coloured. They looked down at their *own images* in the River of Silence, and drew the god Eros from that wave: out of their own self-consciousness, that is. This is a description of the life of introspection and of the love which is begotten by the self in the self, the self-made love. The trees are like serpents worshipping the sun. That is, they represent the phallic passion in its poisonous or mental activity. Everything runs to consciousness: serpents worshipping the sun. The embrace of love, which should bring darkness and oblivion, would with these lovers be a daytime thing bringing more heightened consciousness, visions, spectrum-visions, prismatic. The evil thing that daytime love-making is, and all sex-palaver.

In *Berenice* the man must go down to the sepulchre of his beloved and pull out her thirty-two small white teeth, which he carries in a box with him. It is repulsive and gloating. The teeth are the instruments of biting, of resistance, of antagonism. They often become symbols of opposition, little instruments or entities of crushing and destroying. Hence the dragon's teeth in the myth. Hence the man in *Berenice* must take possession of the irreducible part of his mistress. *"Toutes ses dents étaient des idées,"* he says. Then they are little fixed ideas of mordant hate, of which he possesses himself.

The other great story linking up with this group is *The Fall of the House of Usher.* Here the love is between brother and sister. When the self is broken, and the mystery of the recognition of *otherness* fails, then the longing for identification with the beloved becomes a lust. And it is this longing for identification, utter merging, which is at the base of the incest problem. In psychoanalysis almost every trouble in the psyche is traced to an incest-desire. But it won't do. Incest-desire is only one of the modes by which men strive to get their gratification of the intensest vibration of the spiritual nerves, without any resistance. In the family, the natural vibration is most nearly in unison. With a stranger, there is greater resistance. Incest is the getting of gratification and the avoiding of resistance.

The root of all evil is that we all want this spiritual gratification, this flow, this apparent heightening of life, this knowledge, this valley of many-coloured grass, even grass and light prismatically decomposed, giving ecstasy. We want all this *without resistance.* We want it continually. And this is the root of all evil in us.

We ought to pray to be resisted, and resisted to the bitter end. We ought to decide to have done at last with craving.

The motto to *The Fall of the House of Usher* is a couple of lines from Béranger.

> *"Son cœur est un luth suspendu;*
> *Sitôt qu'on le touche il résonne."*

We have all the trappings of Poe's rather overdone, vulgar fantasy. "I reined my horse to the precipitous brink of a black and lurid tarn that lay in unruffled lustre by the dwelling, and gazed down—but with a shudder even more thrilling than before—upon the remodelled and inverted images of the grey sedge, and the ghastly tree-stems, and the vacant and eye-like windows." The House of Usher, both dwelling and family, was very old. Minute fungi overspread the exterior of the house, hanging in festoons from the eaves. Gothic archways, a valet of stealthy step, sombre tapestries, ebon black floors, a profusion of tattered and antique furniture, feeble gleams of encrimsoned light through latticed panes, and over all "an air of stern, deep, and irredeemable gloom"—this makes up the interior.

The inmates of the house, Roderick and Madeline Usher, are the last remnants of their incomparably ancient and decayed race. Roderick has the same large, luminous eye, the same slightly arched nose of delicate Hebrew model, as characterized Ligeia. He is ill with the nervous malady of his family. It is he whose nerves are so strung that they vibrate to the unknown quiverings of the ether. He, too, has lost his self, his living soul, and become a sensitized instrument of the external influences; his nerves are verily like an æolian harp which must vibrate. He lives in "some struggle with the grim phantasm, Fear," for he is only the physical, post-mortem reality of a living being.

It is a question how much, once the true centrality of the self is broken, the instrumental consciousness of man can register. When man becomes selfless, wafting instrumental like a harp in an open window, how much can his elemental consciousness express? The blood as it runs has its own sympathies and responses to the material world, quite apart from seeing. And the nerves we know vibrate all the while to unseen presences, unseen forces. So Roderick Usher quivers on the edge of material existence.

It is this mechanical consciousness which gives "the fervid facility of his impromptus". It is the same thing that gives Poe his extraordinary facility in versification. The absence of real central or impulsive being in himself leaves him inordinately, mechanically sensitive to sounds and effects, associations of sounds, associations of rhyme, for example—mechanical, facile, having no root in any passion. It is all a secondary, meretricious process. So we get Roderick Usher's poem, *The Haunted Palace*, with its swift yet mechanical subtleties of rhyme and rhythm, its vulgarity of epithet. It is all a sort of dream-process, where the association between parts is mechanical, accidental as far as passional meaning goes.

Usher thought that all vegetable things had sentience. Surely all material things have a *form* of sentience, even the inorganic: surely they all exist in some subtle and complicated tension of vibration which makes them sensitive to external influence and causes them to have an influence on other external objects, irrespective of contact. It is of this vibration or inorganic consciousness that Poe is master: the sleep-consciousness. Thus Roderick Usher was convinced that his whole surroundings, the stones of the house, the fungi, the water in the tarn, the very reflected image of the whole, was woven into a physical oneness with the family, condensed, as it were, into one atmosphere —the special atmosphere in which alone the Ushers could live. And it was this atmosphere which had moulded the destinies of his family.

But while ever the soul remains alive, it is the moulder and not the moulded. It is the souls of living men that subtly impregnate stones, houses, mountains, continents, and give these their subtlest form. People only become subject to stones after having lost their integral souls.

In the human realm, Roderick had one connection: his sister Madeline. She, too, was dying of a mysterious disorder, nervous, cataleptic. The brother and sister loved each other passionately and exclusively. They were twins, almost identical in looks. It was the same absorbing love between them, this process of unison in nerve-vibration, resulting in more and more extreme exaltation and a sort of consciousness, and a gradual break-down into death. The exquisitely sensitive Roger, vibrating without resistance with his sister Madeline, more and more exquisitely, and gradually devouring her, sucking her life like a vampire in his anguish of extreme love. And she asking to be sucked.

Madeline died and was carried down by her brother into the deep vaults of the house. But she was not dead. Her brother roamed about in incipient madness—a madness of unspeakable terror and guilt. After eight days they were suddenly startled by a clash of metal, then a distinct, hollow metallic, and clangorous, yet apparently muffled, reverberation. Then Roderick Usher, gibbering, began to express himself: "*We have put her living in the tomb!* Said I not that my senses were acute? I *now* tell you that I heard her first feeble movements in the hollow coffin. I heard them—many, many days ago—yet I dared not—*I dared not speak.*"

It is the same old theme of "each man kills the thing he loves". He knew his love had killed her. He knew she died at last, like Ligeia, unwilling and unappeased. So, she rose again upon him. "But then without those doors there *did* stand the lofty and enshrouded figure of the lady Madeline of Usher. There was blood upon her white robes, and the evidence of some bitter struggle upon every portion of her emaciated frame. For a moment she remained trembling and reeling to and fro upon the threshold, then, with a low moaning cry, fell heavily inward upon the person of her brother, and in her violent and now final death-agonies bore him to the floor a corpse, and a victim to the terrors he had anticipated."

It is lurid and melodramatic, but it is true. It is a ghastly psychological truth of what happens in the last stages of this beloved love, which cannot be separate, cannot be isolate, cannot listen in isolation to the isolate Holy Ghost. For it is the Holy Ghost we must live by. The next era is the era of the Holy Ghost. And the Holy Ghost speaks individually inside each individual : always, for ever a ghost. There is no manifestation to the general world. Each isolate individual listening in isolation to the Holy Ghost within him.

The Ushers, brother and sister, betrayed the Holy Ghost in themselves. They would love, love, love, without resistance. They would love, they would merge, they would be as one thing. So they dragged each other down into death. For the Holy Ghost says you must *not* be as one thing with another being. Each must abide by itself, and correspond only within certain limits.

The best tales all have the same burden. Hate is as inordinate as love, and as slowly consuming, as secret, as underground, as subtle. All this underground vault business in Poe only symbolizes that which takes place *beneath* the consciousness. On top, all is fair-spoken. Beneath, there is awful murderous extremity of burying alive. Fortunato, in *The Cask of Amontillado*, is buried alive out of perfect hatred, as the lady Madeline of Usher is buried alive out of love. The lust of hate is the inordinate desire to consume and unspeakably possess the soul of the hated one, just as the lust of love is the desire to possess, or to be possessed by, the beloved, utterly. But in either case the result is the dissolution of both souls, each losing itself in transgressing its own bounds.

The lust of Montresor is to devour utterly the soul of Fortunato. It would be no use killing him outright. If a man is killed outright his soul remains integral, free to return into the bosom of some beloved, where it can enact itself. In walling-up his enemy in the vault, Montresor seeks to bring about the indescribable capitulation of the man's soul, so that he, the victor, can possess himself of the very being of the vanquished. Perhaps this can actually be done. Perhaps, in the attempt, the victor breaks the bonds of his own identity, and collapses into nothingness, or into the infinite. Becomes a monster.

What holds good for inordinate hate holds good for inordinate love. The motto, *Nemo me impune lacessit*, might just as well be *Nemo me impune amat*.

In *William Wilson* we are given a rather unsubtle account of the attempt of a man to kill his own soul. William Wilson the mechanical, lustful ego succeeds in killing William Wilson the living self. The lustful ego lives on, gradually reducing itself towards the dust of the infinite.

In the *Murders in the Rue Morgue* and *The Gold Bug* we have those mechanical tales where the interest lies in the following out of a subtle chain of cause and effect. The interest is scientific rather than artistic, a study in psychologic reactions.

The fascination of murder itself is curious. Murder is not just killing. Murder is a lust to get at the very quick of life itself, and kill it—hence the stealth and the frequent morbid dismemberment of the corpse, the attempt to get at the very quick of the murdered being, to find the quick and to possess it. It is curious that the two men fascinated by the art of murder, though in different ways, should have been De Quincey and Poe, men so different in ways of life, yet perhaps not so widely different in nature. In each of them is traceable that strange lust for extreme love and extreme hate, possession by mystic violence of the other soul, or violent deathly surrender of the soul in the self: an absence of manly virtue, which stands alone and accepts limits.

Inquisition and torture are akin to murder: the same lust. It is a combat between inquisitor and victim as to whether the inquisitor shall get at the quick of life itself, and pierce it. Pierce the very quick of the soul. The evil will of man tries to do this. The brave soul of man refuses to have the life-quick pierced in him. It is strange: but just as the thwarted will can persist evilly, after death, so can the brave spirit preserve, even through torture and death, the quick of life and truth. Nowadays society is evil. It finds subtle ways of torture, to destroy the life-quick, to get at the life-quick in a man. Every possible form. And still a man can hold out, if he can laugh and listen to the Holy Ghost.—But society is evil, evil, and love is evil. And evil breeds evil, more and more.

So the mystery goes on. La Bruyère says that all our human unhappiness *viennent de ne pouvoir être seuls*. As long as man lives he will be subject to the yearning of love or the burning of hate, which is only inverted love.

But he is subject to something more than this. If we do not live to eat, we do not live to love either.

We live to stand alone, and listen to the Holy Ghost. The Holy Ghost, who is inside us, and who is many gods. Many gods come and go, some say one thing and some say another, and we have to obey the God of the innermost hour. It is the multiplicity of gods within us make up the Holy Ghost.

But Poe knew only love, love, love, intense vibrations and heightened consciousness. Drugs, women, self-destruction, but anyhow the prismatic ecstasy of heightened consciousness and sense of love, of flow. The human soul in him was beside itself. But it was not lost. He told us plainly how it was, so that we should know.

He was an adventurer into vaults and cellars and horrible underground passages of the human soul. He sounded the horror and the warning of his own doom.

Doomed he was. He died wanting more love, and love killed him. A ghastly disease, love. Poe telling us of his disease: trying even to make his disease fair and attractive. Even succeeding.

Which is the inevitable falseness, duplicity of art, American art in particular.

CHAPTER VII

NATHANIEL HAWTHORNE AND "THE SCARLET LETTER"

NATHANIEL HAWTHORNE writes romance.

And what's romance? Usually, a nice little tale where you have everything As You Like It, where rain never wets your jacket and gnats never bite your nose and it's always daisy-time. *As You Like It* and *Forest Lovers*, etc. *Morte D'Arthur*.

Hawthorne obviously isn't this kind of romanticist: though nobody has muddy boots in *The Scarlet Letter*, either.

But there is more to it. *The Scarlet Letter* isn't a pleasant, pretty romance. It is a sort of parable, an earthly story with a hellish meaning.

All the time there is this split in the American art and art-consciousness. On the top it is as nice as pie, goody-goody and lovey-dovey. Like Hawthorne being such a blue-eyed darling, in life, and Longfellow and the rest such sucking-doves. Hawthorne's wife said she "never saw him in time", which doesn't mean she saw him too late. But always in the "frail effulgence of eternity"

Serpents they were. Look at the inner meaning of their art and see what demons they were.

You *must* look through the surface of American art, and see the inner diabolism of the symbolic meaning. Otherwise it is all mere childishness.

That blue-eyed darling Nathaniel knew disagreeable things in his inner soul. He was careful to send them out in disguise.

Always the same. The deliberate consciousness of Americans so fair and smooth-spoken, and the under-consciousness so devilish. *Destroy! destroy! destroy!* hums the under-consciousness. *Love and produce! Love and produce!* cackles the upper consciousness. And the world hears only the Love-and-produce cackle. Refuses to hear the hum of destruction underneath. Until such time as it will *have* to hear.

The American has got to destroy. It is his destiny. It is his destiny to destroy the whole corpus of the white psyche, the white consciousness. And he's got to do it secretly. As the growing of a dragon-fly inside a chrysalis or cocoon destroys the larva grub, secretly.

Though many a dragon-fly never gets out of the chrysalis case: dies inside. As America might.

So the secret chrysalis of *The Scarlet Letter*, diabolically destroying the old psyche inside.

Be good! Be good! warbles Nathaniel. *Be good, and never sin! Be sure your sins will find you out.*

So convincingly that his wife never saw him "as in time".

Then listen to the diabolic undertone of *The Scarlet Letter*.

Man ate of the tree of knowledge, and became ashamed of himself.

Do you imagine Adam had never lived with Eve before that apple episode? Yes, he had. As a wild animal with his mate.

It didn't become "sin" till the knowledge-poison entered. That apple of Sodom.

We are divided in ourselves, against ourselves. And that is the meaning of the cross symbol.

In the first place, Adam knew Eve as a wild animal knows its mate, momentaneously, but vitally, in blood-knowledge. Blood-knowledge, not mind-knowledge. Blood-knowledge, that seems utterly to forget, but doesn't. Blood-knowledge, instinct, intuition, all the vast vital flux of knowing that goes on in the dark, antecedent to the mind.

Then came that beastly apple, and the other sort of knowledge started.

Adam began to look at himself. "My hat!" he said. "What's this? My Lord! What the deuce!—And Eve! I wonder about Eve."

Thus starts KNOWING. Which shortly runs to UNDERSTANDING, when the devil gets his own.

When Adam went and took Eve, *after* the apple, he didn't do any more than he had done many a time before, in act. But in consciousness he did something very different.

So did Eve. Each of them kept an eye on what they were doing, they watched what was happening to them. They wanted to KNOW. And that was the birth of sin. Not *doing* it, but KNOWING about it. Before the apple, they had shut their eyes and their minds had gone dark. Now, they peeped and pried and imagined. They watched themselves. And they felt uncomfortable after. They felt self-conscious. So they said, "The *act* is sin. Let's hide. We've sinned."

No wonder the Lord kicked them out of the Garden. Dirty hypocrites.

The sin was the self-watching, self-consciousness. The sin, and the doom. Dirty understanding.

Nowadays men do hate the idea of dualism. It's no good, dual we are. The cross. If we accept the symbol, then, virtually, we accept the fact. We are divided against ourselves.

For instance, the blood *hates* being KNOWN by the mind. It feels itself destroyed when it is KNOWN. Hence the profound instinct of privacy.

And on the other hand, the mind and the spiritual consciousness of man simply *hates* the dark potency of blood-acts: hates the genuine dark sensual orgasms, which do, for the time being, actually obliterate the mind and the spiritual consciousness, plunge them in a suffocating flood of darkness.

You can't get away from this.

Blood-consciousness overwhelms, obliterates, and annuls mind-consciousness.

Mind-consciousness extinguishes blood-consciousness, and consumes the blood.

We are all of us conscious in both ways. And the two ways are antagonistic in us.

They will always remain so.

That is our cross.

The antagonism is so obvious, and so far-reaching, that it extends to the smallest thing. The cultured, highly-conscious person of to-day *loathes* any form of physical, "menial" work: such as washing dishes or sweeping a floor or chopping wood. This menial work is an insult to the spirit. "When I see men carrying heavy loads, doing brutal work, it always makes me want to cry," said a beautiful, cultured woman to me.

"When you say that, it makes me want to beat you," said I, in reply. "When I see you with your beautiful head pondering heavy thoughts, I just want to hit you. It outrages me."

My father hated books, hated the sight of anyone reading or writing.

My mother hated the thought that any of her sons should be condemned to manual labour. Her sons must have something higher than that.

She won. But she died first.

He laughs longest who laughs last.

There is a basic hostility in all of us between the physical and the mental, the blood and the spirit. The mind is "ashamed" of the blood. And the blood is destroyed by the mind, actually. Hence pale-faces.

At present the mind-consciousness and the so-called spirit triumphs. In America supremely. In America, nobody does anything from the blood. Always from the nerves, if not from the mind. The blood is chemically reduced by the nerves, in American activity.

When an Italian labourer labours, his mind and nerves sleep, his blood acts ponderously.

Americans, when they are *doing* things, never seem really to be doing them. They are "busy about" it. They are always busy "about" something. But truly *immersed* in *doing* something, with the deep blood-consciousness active, that they never are.

They *admire* the blood-conscious spontaneity. And they want to get it in their heads. "Live from the body," they shriek. It is their last mental shriek. *Co-ordinate.*

It is a further attempt still to rationalize the body and blood. "Think about such and such a muscle," they say, "and relax there."

And every time you "conquer" the body with the mind (you can say "heal" it, if you like) you cause a deeper, more dangerous complex or tension somewhere else.

Ghastly Americans, with their blood no longer blood. A yellow spiritual fluid.

The Fall.

There have been lots of Falls.

We *fell* into *knowledge* when Eve bit the apple. Self-conscious knowledge. For the first time the mind put up a fight against the blood. Wanting to UNDERSTAND. That is to intellectualize the blood.

The blood must be *shed*, says Jesus.

Shed on the cross of our own divided psyche.

Shed the blood, and you become mind-conscious. Eat the body and drink the blood, self-cannibalizing, and you become extremely conscious, like Americans and some Hindus. Devour yourself, and God knows what a lot you'll know, what a lot you'll be conscious of.

Mind you don't choke yourself.

For a long time men *believed* that they could be perfected through the mind, through the spirit. They believed, passionately. They had their ecstasy in pure consciousness. They *believed* in purity, chastity, and the wings of the spirit.

America soon plucked the bird of the spirit. America soon killed the *belief* in the spirit. But not the practice. The practice continued with a sarcastic vehemence. America, with a perfect inner contempt for the spirit and the consciousness of man, practises the same spirituality and universal love and KNOWING all the time, incessantly, like a drug habit. And inwardly gives not a fig for it. Only for the *sensation*. The pretty-pretty *sensation* of love, loving all the world. And the nice fluttering aeroplane *sensation* of knowing, knowing, knowing. Then the prettiest of all sensations, the sensation of UNDERSTANDING. Oh, what a lot they understand, the darlings! *So* good at the trick, they are. Just a trick of self-conceit.

The Scarlet Letter gives the show away.

You have your pure-pure young parson Dimmesdale.

You have the beautiful Puritan Hester at his feet.

And the first thing she does is to seduce him.

And the first thing he does is to be seduced.

And the second thing they do is to hug their sin in secret, and gloat over it, and try to understand.

Which is the myth of New England.

Deerslayer refused to be seduced by Judith Hutter. At least the Sodom apple of sin didn't fetch him.

But Dimmesdale was seduced gloatingly. Oh, luscious Sin!

He was such a pure young man.

That he had to make a fool of purity.

The American psyche.

Of course, the best part of the game lay in keeping up pure appearances.

The greatest triumph a woman can have, especially an American woman, is the triumph of seducing a man: especially if he is pure.

And he gets the greatest thrill of all, in falling.—"Seduce me, Mrs. Hercules."

And the pair of them share the subtlest delight in keeping up pure appearances, when everybody knows all the while. But the power of pure appearances is something to exult in. All America gives in to it. *Look* pure!

To seduce a man. To have everybody know. To keep up appearances of purity. Pure!

This is the great triumph of woman.

A. The Scarlet Letter. Adulteress! The great Alpha. Alpha! Adulteress! The new Adam and Adama! American!

A. Adulteress! Stitched with gold thread, glittering upon the bosom. The proudest insignia.

Put her upon the scaffold and worship her there. Worship her there. The Woman, the Magna Mater. *A.* Adulteress! Abel!

Abel! Abel! Abel! Admirable!

It becomes a farce.

The fiery heart. *A.* Mary of the Bleeding Heart. Mater Adolerata! *A.* Capital *A.* Adulteress. Glittering with gold thread. Abel! Adultery. Admirable!

It is, perhaps, the most colossal satire ever penned. *The Scarlet Letter*. And by a blue-eyed darling of a Nathaniel.

Not Bumppo, however.

The human spirit, fixed in a lie, adhering to a lie, giving itself perpetually the lie.

All begins with *A*.

Adulteress. Alpha. Abel, Adam. *A.* America.

The Scarlet Letter.

"Had there been a Papist among the crowd of Puritans, he might have seen in this beautiful woman, so picturesque in her attire and mien, and with the infant at her bosom, an object to remind him of the image of Divine Maternity, which so many illustrious painters have vied with one another to represent; something which should remind him, indeed, but only by contrast, of that sacred image of sinless Motherhood, whose infant was to redeem the world."

Whose infant was to redeem the world indeed! It will be a startling redemption the world will get from the American infant.

"Here was a taint of deepest sin in the most sacred quality of human life, working such effect that the world was only the darker for this woman's beauty, and more lost for the infant she had borne."

Just listen to the darling. Isn't he a master of apology?

Of symbols, too.

His pious blame is a chuckle of praise all the while.

Oh, Hester, you are a demon. A man *must* be pure, just so that you can seduce him to a fall. Because the greatest thrill in life is to bring down the Sacred Saint with a flop into the mud. Then when you've brought him down, humbly wipe off the mud with your hair, another Magdalen. And then go home and dance a witch's jig of triumph, and stitch yourself a Scarlet Letter with gold thread, as duchesses used to stitch themselves coronets. And then stand meek on the scaffold and fool the world. Who will all be envying you your sin, and beating you because you've stolen an advantage over them.

Hester Prynne is the great nemesis of woman. She is the KNOWING Ligeia risen diabolic from the grave. Having her own back. UNDERSTANDING.

This time it is Mr. Dimmesdale who dies. She lives on and is Abel.

His spiritual love was a lie. And prostituting the woman to his spiritual love, as popular clergymen do, in his preachings and loftiness, was a tall white lie. Which came flop.

We are so pure in spirit. Hi-tiddly-i-ty!

Till she tickled him in the right place, and he fell.

Flop.

Flop goes spiritual love.

But keep up the game. Keep up appearances. Pure are the pure. To the pure all things, etc.

Look out, Mister, for the Female Devotee. Whatever you do, don't let her start tickling you. She knows your weak spot. Mind your Purity.

When Hester Prynne seduced Arthur Dimmesdale it was the beginning of the end. But from the beginning of the end to the end of the end is a hundred years or two.

Mr. Dimmesdale also wasn't at the end of his resources. Previously, he had lived by governing his body, ruling it, in the interests of his spirit. Now he has a good time all by himself torturing his body, whipping it, piercing it with thorns, macerating himself. It's a form of masturbation. He wants to get a mental grip on his body. And since he can't quite manage it with the mind, witness his fall—he will give it what for, with whips. His will shall *lash* his body. And he enjoys his pains. Wallows in them. To the pure all things are pure.

It is the old self-mutilation process, gone rotten. The mind wanting to get its teeth in the blood and flesh. The ego exulting in the tortures of the mutinous flesh. I, the ego, I *will* triumph over my own flesh. Lash! Lash! I am a grand free spirit. *Lash!* I am the master of my soul! *Lash! Lash!* I am the captain of my soul. *Lash!* Hurray! "In the fell clutch of circumstance," etc., etc.

Good-bye Arthur. He depended on women for his Spiritual Devotees, spiritual brides. So, the woman just touched him in his weak spot, his Achilles Heel of the flesh. Look out for the spiritual bride. She's after the weak spot.

It is the battle of wills.

"For the will therein lieth, which dieth not——"

The Scarlet Woman becomes a Sister of Mercy. Didn't she just, in the late war. Oh, Prophet Nathaniel!

Hester urges Dimmesdale to go away with her, to a new country, to a new life. He isn't having any.

He knows there is no new country, no new life on the globe to-day. It is the same old thing, in different degrees, everywhere. *Plus ça change, plus c'est la même chose.*

Hester thinks, with Dimmesdale for her husband, and Pearl for her child, in Australia, maybe, she'd have been perfect.

But she wouldn't. Dimmesdale had already fallen from his integrity as a minister of the Gospel of the Spirit. He had lost his manliness. He didn't see the point of just leaving himself between the hands of a woman and going away to a "new country", to be her thing entirely. She'd only have despised him more, as every woman despises a man who has "fallen" to her; despises him with her tenderest lust.

He stood for nothing any more. So let him stay where he was and dree out his weird.

She had dished him and his spirituality, so he hated her. As Angel Clare was dished, and hated Tess. As Jude in the end hated Sue: or should have done. The women make fools of them, the spiritual men. And when, as men, they've gone flop in their spirituality, they can't pick themselves up whole any more. So they just crawl, and die detesting the female, or the females, who made them fall.

The saintly minister gets a bit of his own back, at the last minute, by making public confession from the very scaffold where she was exposed. Then he dodges into death. But he's had a bit of his own back, on everybody.

" 'Shall we not meet again?' whispered she, bending her face down close to him. 'Shall we not spend our immortal life together? Surely, surely we have ransomed one another with all this woe! Thou lookest far into eternity with those bright dying eyes. Tell me what thou seest!' "

" 'Hush, Hester—hush,' said he, with tremulous solemnity. 'The law we broke!—the sin here so awfully revealed! Let these alone be in thy thoughts. I fear! I fear!' "

So he dies, throwing the "sin" in her teeth, and escaping into death.

The law we broke, indeed. You bet!

Whose law!

But it is truly a law, that man must either stick to the belief he has grounded himself on, and obey the laws of that belief, or he must admit the belief itself to be inadequate, and prepare himself for a new thing.

There was no change in belief, either in Hester or in Dimmesdale or in Hawthorne or in America. The same old treacherous belief, which was really cunning disbelief, in the Spirit, in Purity, in Selfless Love, and in Pure Consciousness. They would go on following this belief, for the sake of the sensationalism of it. But they would make a fool of it all the time. Like Woodrow Wilson, and the rest of modern Believers. The rest of modern Saviours.

If you meet a Saviour, to-day, be sure he is trying to make an innermost fool of you. Especially if the saviour be an UNDERSTANDING WOMAN, offering her love.

Hester lives on, pious as pie, being a public nurse. She becomes at last an acknowledged saint, Abel of the Scarlet Letter.

She would, being a woman. She has had her triumph

over the individual man, so she quite loves subscribing to the whole spiritual life of society. She will make herself as false as hell, for society's sake, once she's had her real triumph over Saint Arthur.

Blossoms out into a Sister-of-Mercy Saint.

But it's a long time before she really takes anybody in. People kept on thinking her a witch, which she was.

As a matter of fact, unless a woman is held, by man, safe within the bounds of belief, she becomes inevitably a destructive force. She can't help herself. A woman is almost always vulnerable to pity. She can't bear to see anything *physically* hurt. But let a woman loose from the bounds and restraints of man's fierce belief, in his gods and in himself, and she becomes a gentle devil. She becomes subtly diabolic. The colossal evil of the united spirit of Woman. WOMAN, German woman or American woman, or every other sort of woman, in the last war, was something frightening. As every *man* knows.

Woman becomes a helpless, would-be-loving demon. She is helpless. Her very love is a subtle poison.

Unless a man believes in himself and his gods, *genuinely*: unless he fiercely obeys his own Holy Ghost; his woman will destroy him. Woman is the nemesis of doubting man. She can't help it.

And with Hester, after Ligeia, woman becomes a nemesis to man. She bolsters him up from the outside, she destroys him from the inside. And he dies hating her, as Dimmesdale did.

Dimmesdale's spirituality had gone on too long, too far. It had become a false thing. He found his nemesis in woman. And he was done for.

Woman is a strange and rather terrible phenomenon, to man. When the subconscious soul of woman recoils from its creative union with man, it becomes a destructive force. It exerts, willy-nilly, an invisible destructive influence. The woman herself may be as nice as milk, to all appearance, like Ligeia. But she is sending out waves of silent destruction of the faltering spirit in men, all the same. She doesn't know it. She can't even help it. But she does it. The devil is in her.

The very women who are most busy saving the bodies of

men, and saving the children: these women-doctors, these nurses, these educationalists, these public-spirited women, these female saviours: they are all, from the inside, sending out waves of destructive malevolence which eat out the inner life of a man, like a cancer. It is so, it will be so, till men realize it and react to save themselves.

God won't save us. The women are so devilish godly. Men must save themselves in this strait, and by no sugary means either.

A woman can use her sex in sheer malevolence and poison, while she is *behaving* as meek and good as gold. Dear darling, she is really snow-white in her blamelessness. And all the while she is using her sex as a she-devil, for the endless hurt of her man. She doesn't know it. She will never believe it if you tell her. And if you give her a slap in the face for her fiendishness, she will rush to the first magistrate, in indignation. She is so *absolutely* blameless, the she-devil, the dear, dutiful creature.

Give her the great slap, just the same, just when she is being most angelic. Just when she is bearing her cross most meekly.

Oh, woman out of bounds is a devil. But it is man's fault. Woman never *asked*, in the first place, to be cast out of her bit of an Eden of belief and trust. It is man's business to bear the responsibility of belief. If he becomes a spiritual fornicator and liar, like Ligeia's husband and Arthur Dimmesdale, how *can* a woman believe in him? Belief doesn't go by choice. And if a woman doesn't believe in a *man*, she believes, essentially, in nothing. She becomes, willy-nilly, a devil.

A devil she is, and a devil she will be. And most men will succumb to her devilishness.

Hester Prynne was a devil. Even when she was so meekly going round as a sick-nurse. Poor Hester. Part of her wanted to be saved from her own devilishness. And another part wanted to go on and on in devilishness, for revenge. Revenge! REVENGE! It is this that fills the unconscious spirit of woman to-day. Revenge against man, and against the spirit of man, which has betrayed her into unbelief. Even when she is most sweet and a salvationist, she is her most devilish, is woman. She gives her man the sugar-plum of her own submissive sweetness. And when he's taken this sugar-plum in his mouth, a scorpion comes out of it. After he's taken this Eve to his bosom, oh, so loving, she destroys him inch by inch. Woman and her revenge! She will have it, and go on having it, for decades and decades, unless she's stopped. And to stop her you've got to believe in yourself and your gods, your own Holy Ghost, Sir Man; and then you've got to fight her, and never give in. She's a devil. But in the long run she is conquerable. And just a tiny bit of her wants to be conquered. You've got to fight three-quarters of her, in absolute hell, to get at the final quarter of her that wants a release, at last, from the hell of her own revenge. But it's a long last. And not yet.

"She had in her nature a rich, voluptuous, oriental characteristic—a taste for the gorgeously beautiful." This is Hester. This is American. But she repressed her nature in the above direction. She would not even allow herself the luxury of labouring at fine, delicate stitching. Only she dressed her little sin-child Pearl vividly, and the scarlet letter was gorgeously embroidered. Her Hecate and Astarte insignia.

"A voluptuous, oriental characteristic——" That lies waiting in American women. It is probable that the Mormons are the forerunners of the coming real America. It is probable that men will have more than one wife, in the coming America. That you will have again a half-oriental womanhood, and a polygamy.

The grey nurse, Hester. The Hecate, the hell-cat. The slowly-evolving voluptuous female of the new era, with a whole new submissiveness to the dark, phallic principle.

But it takes time. Generation after generation of nurses and political women and salvationists. And in the end, the dark erection of the images of sex-worship once more, and the newly submissive women. That kind of depth. Deep women in that respect. When we have at last broken this insanity of mental-spiritual consciousness. And the women *choose* to experience again the great submission.

"The poor, whom she sought out to be the objects of her bounty, often reviled the hand that was stretched to succour them."

Naturally. The poor hate a salvationist. They smell the devil underneath.

"She was patient—a martyr indeed—but she forbore to

pray for her enemies, lest, in spite of her forgiving aspira-
tions, the words of the blessing should stubbornly twist
themselves into a curse."

So much honesty, at least. No wonder the old witch-lady
Mistress Hibbins claimed her for another witch.

"She grew to have a dread of children; for they had
imbibed from their parents a vague idea of something horrible in this dreary woman gliding silently through the
town, with never any companion but only one child."

"A vague idea!" Can't you see her "gliding silently"?
It's not a question of a vague idea imbibed, but a definite
feeling directly received.

"But sometimes, once in many days, or perchance in
many months, she felt an eye—a human eye—upon the
ignominious brand, that seemed to give a momentary relief,
as if half her agony were shared. The next instant, back it
all rushed again, with a still deeper throb of pain; for in
that brief interval she had sinned again. Had Hester sinned
alone?"

Of course not. As for sinning again, she would go on all
her life silently, changelessly "sinning". She never repented.
Not she. Why should she? She had brought down Arthur
Dimmesdale, that too-too snow-white bird, and that was
her life-work.

As for sinning again when she met two dark eyes in a
crowd, why, of course. Somebody who understood as she
understood.

I always remember meeting the eyes of a gipsy woman,
for one moment, in a crowd, in England. She knew, and I
knew. What did we know? I was not able to make out. But
we knew.

Probably the same fathomless hate of this spiritual-con-
scious society in which the outcast woman and I both
roamed like meek-looking wolves. Tame wolves waiting to
shake off their tameness. Never able to.

And again, that "voluptuous, oriental" characteristic that
knows the mystery of the ithyphallic gods. She would not
betray the ithyphallic gods to this white, leprous-white
society of "lovers". Neither will I, if I can help it. These
leprous-white, seducing, spiritual women, who "understand" so much. One has been too often seduced, and
"understood". "I can read him like a book," said my first

lover of me. The book is in several volumes, dear. And more and more comes back to me the gulf of dark hate and *other* understanding, in the eyes of the gipsy woman. So different from the hateful white light of understanding which floats like scum on the eyes of white, oh, so white English· and American women, with their understanding voices and their deep, sad words, and their profound, *good* spirits. Pfui!

Hester was scared only of one result of her sin: Pearl. Pearl, the scarlet letter incarnate. The little girl. When women bear children, they produce either devils or sons with gods in them. And it is an evolutionary process. The devil in Hester produced a purer devil in Pearl. And the devil in Pearl will produce—she married an Italian Count —a piece of purer devilishness still.

And so from hour to hour we ripe and ripe.

And then from hour to hour we rot and rot.

There was that in the child "which often impelled Hester to ask in bitterness of heart, whether it were for good or ill that the poor little creature had been born at all".

For ill, Hester. But don't worry. Ill is as necessary as good. Malevolence is as necessary as benevolence. If you have brought forth, spawned, a young malevolence, be sure there is a rampant falseness in the world against which this malevolence must be turned. Falseness has to be bitten and bitten, till it is bitten to death. Hence Pearl.

Pearl. Her own mother compares her to the demon of plague, or scarlet fever, in her red dress. But then, plague is necessary to destroy a rotten, false humanity.

Pearl, the devilish girl-child, who can be so tender and loving and *understanding*, and then, when she has understood, will give you a hit across the mouth, and turn on you with a grin of sheer diabolic jeering.

Serves you right, you shouldn't be *understood*. That is your vice. You shouldn't want to be loved, and then you'd not get hit across the mouth. Pearl will love you: marvellously. And she'll hit you across the mouth: oh, so neatly. And serves you right.

Pearl is perhaps the most modern child in all literature.

Old-fashioned Nathaniel, with his little-boy charm, he'll tell you what's what. But he'll cover it with smarm.

Hester simply *hates* her child, from one part of herself.

And from another, she cherishes her child as her one precious treasure. For Pearl is the continuing of her female revenge on life. But female revenge hits both ways. Hits back at its own mother. The female revenge in Pearl hits back at Hester, the mother, and Hester is simply livid with fury and "sadness", which is rather amusing.

"The child could not be made amenable to rules. In giving her existence a great law had been broken; and the result was a being whose elements were perhaps beautiful and brilliant, but all in disorder, or with an order peculiar to themselves, amidst which the point of variety and arrangement was difficult or impossible to discover."

Of course, the order is peculiar to themselves. But the point of variety is this: "Draw out the loving, sweet soul, draw it out with marvellous understanding; and then spit in its eye."

Hester, of course, didn't at all like it when her sweet child drew out her motherly soul, with yearning and deep understanding: and then spit in the motherly eye, with a grin. But it was a process the mother had started.

Pearl had a peculiar look in her eyes: "a look so intelligent, yet so inexplicable, so perverse, sometimes so malicious, but generally accompanied by a wild flow of spirits, that Hester could not help questioning at such moments whether Pearl was a human child."

A little demon! But her mother, and the saintly Dimmesdale, had borne her. And Pearl, by the very openness of her perversity, was more straightforward than her parents. She flatly refuses any Heavenly Father, seeing the earthly one such a fraud. And she has the pietistic Dimmesdale on toast, spits right in his eye: in both his eyes.

Poor, brave, tormented little soul, always in a state of recoil, she'll be a devil to men when she grows up. But the men deserve it. If they'll let themselves be "drawn", by her loving understanding, they deserve that she shall slap them across the mouth the moment they *are* drawn. The chickens! Drawn and trussed.

Poor little phenomenon of a modern child, she'll grow up into the devil of a modern woman. The nemesis of weak-kneed modern men, craving to be love-drawn.

The third person in the diabolic trinity, or triangle, of

the Scarlet Letter, is Hester's first husband, Roger Chilling-
worth. He is an old Elizabethan physician, with a grey
beard and a long-furred coat and a twisted shoulder.
Another healer. But something of an alchemist, a magician.
He is a magician on the verge of modern science, like
Francis Bacon.

Roger Chillingworth is of the old order of intellect, in
direct line from the mediæval Roger Bacon alchemists. He
has an old, intellectual belief in the dark sciences, the Her-
metic philosophies. He is no Christian, no selfless aspirer.
He is not an aspirer. He is the old authoritarian in man.
The old male authority. But without passional belief. Only
intellectual belief in himself and his male authority.

Shakespeare's whole tragic wail is because of the down-
fall of the true male authority, the ithyphallic authority
and masterhood. It fell with Elizabeth. It was trodden
underfoot with Victoria.

But Chillingworth keeps on the *intellectual* tradition. He
hates the new spiritual aspirers, like Dimmesdale, with a
black, crippled hate. He is the old male authority, in intellectual tradition.

You can't keep a wife by force of an intellectual tradition. So Hester took to seducing Dimmesdale.

Yet her only marriage, and her last oath, is with the old
Roger. He and she are accomplices in pulling down the
spiritual saint.

"Why dost thou smile so at me—" she says to her old,
vengeful husband. "Art thou not like the Black Man that
haunts the forest around us? Hast thou not enticed me
into a bond which will prove the ruin of my soul?"

"Not thy soul!" he answered with another smile. "No,
not thy soul!"

It is the soul of the pure preacher, that false thing, which
they are after. And the crippled physician—this other
healer—blackly vengeful in his old, distorted male authority, and the "loving" woman, they bring down the saint
between them.

A black and complementary hatred, akin to love, is what
Chillingworth feels for the young, saintly parson. And
Dimmesdale responds, in a hideous kind of love. Slowly the
saint's life is poisoned. But the black old physician smiles,
and tries to keep him alive. Dimmesdale goes in for self-

torture, self-lashing, lashing his own white, thin, spiritual saviour's body. The dark old Chillingworth listens outside the door and laughs, and prepares another medicine, so that the game can go on longer. And the saint's very soul goes rotten. Which is the supreme triumph. Yet he keeps up appearances still.

The black, vengeful soul of the crippled, masterful male, still dark in his authority: and the white ghastliness of the fallen saint! The two halves of manhood mutually destroying one another.

Dimmesdale has a "coup" in the very end. He gives the whole show away by confessing publicly on the scaffold, and dodging into death, leaving Hester dished, and Roger as it were, doubly cuckolded. It is a neat last revenge.

Down comes the curtain, as in Ligeia's poem.

But the child Pearl will be on in the next act, with her Italian Count and a new brood of vipers. And Hester greyly Abelling, in the shadows, after her rebelling.

It is a marvellous allegory. It is to me one of the greatest allegories in all literature, *The Scarlet Letter*. Its marvellous under-meaning! And its perfect duplicity.

The absolute duplicity of that blue-eyed *Wunderkind* of a Nathaniel. The American wonder-child, with his magical allegorical insight.

But even wonder-children have to grow up in a generation or two.

And even SIN becomes stale.

CHAPTER VIII

HAWTHORNE'S "BLITHEDALE ROMANCE"

No other book of Nathaniel Hawthorne is so deep, so dual, and so complete as *The Scarlet Letter*: this great allegory of the triumph of sin.

Sin is a queer thing. It isn't the breaking of divine commandments. It is the breaking of one's own integrity.

For instance, the sin in Hester and Arthur Dimmesdale's case was a sin because they did what they *thought* it *wrong* to do. If they had really *wanted* to be lovers, and if they had had the honest courage of their own passion, there would have been no sin, even had the desire been only momentary.

But if there had been no sin, they would have lost half the fun, or more, of the game.

It was this very doing of the thing that *they themselves* believed to be wrong, that constituted the chief charm of the act. Man invents sin, in order to enjoy the feeling of being naughty. Also, in order to shift the responsibility for his own acts. A Divine Father tells him what to do. And man is naughty and doesn't obey. And then shiveringly, ignoble man lets down his pants for a flogging.

If the Divine Father doesn't bring on the flogging, in this life, then Sinful Man shiveringly awaits his whipping in the afterlife.

Bah, the Divine Father, like so many other Crowned Heads, has abdicated his authority. Man can sin as much as he likes.

There is only one penalty: the loss of his own integrity. Man should *never* do the thing he believes to be wrong. Because if he does, he loses his own singleness, wholeness, natural honour.

If you want to do a thing, you've either got to believe, sincerely, that it's your true nature to do this thing—or else you've got to let it alone.

Believe in your own Holy Ghost. Or else, if you doubt, abstain.

A thing that you sincerely believe in cannot be wrong, because belief does not come at will. It comes only from the Holy Ghost within. Therefore a thing you truly believe in, cannot be wrong.

But there is such a thing as spurious belief. There is such a thing as *evil* belief: a belief that one *cannot do wrong*. There is also such a thing as a half-spurious belief. And this is rottenest of all. The devil lurking behind the cross.

So there you are. Between genuine belief, and spurious belief, and half-genuine belief, you're as likely as not to be in a pickle. And the half-genuine belief is much the dirtiest, and most deceptive thing in life.

Hester and Dimmesdale believed in the Divine Father, and almost gloatingly sinned against Him. The Allegory of Sin.

Pearl no longer believes in the Divine Father. She says so. She has no Divine Father. Disowns Papa both big and little.

So she can't sin against him.

What will she do, then, if she's got no god to sin against? Why, of course, she'll not be able to sin at all. She'll go her own way gaily, and do as she likes, and she'll say, afterwards, when she's made a mess: "Yes, I did it. But I acted for the best, and therefore I am blameless. It's the other person's fault. Or else it's Its fault."

She will be blameless, will Pearl, come what may.

And the world is simply a string of Pearls to-day. And America is a whole rope of these absolutely immaculate Pearls, who can't sin, let them do what they may, because they've no god to sin against. Mere men, one after another. Men with no ghost to their name.

Pearls!

Oh, the irony, the bitter, bitter irony of the name! Oh, Nathaniel, you great man! Oh, America, you Pearl, you Pearl without a blemish!

How *can* Pearl have a blemish, when there's no one but herself to judge Herself? Of course she'll be immaculate, even if, like Cleopatra, she drowns a lover a night in her dirty Nile. The Nilus Flux of her love.

Candida!

By Hawthorne's day it was already Pearl. Before swine,

of course. There never yet was a Pearl that wasn't cast before swine.

It's part of her game, part of her pearldom.

Because when Circe lies with a man, *he*'s a swine after it, if he wasn't one before. Not *she*. Circe is the great white impeccable Pearl.

And yet, oh, Pearl, there's a Nemesis even for you.

There's a Doom, Pearl.

Doom! What a beautiful northern word. Doom.

The doom of the Pearl.

Who will write that Allegory?

Here's what the Doom is, anyhow.

When you don't have a Divine Father to sin against; and when you don't sin against the Son; which the Pearls don't, because they all are very strong on LOVE, stronger on LOVE than on anything: then there's nothing left for you to sin against except the Holy Ghost.

Now, Pearl, come, let's drop you in the vinegar.

And it's a ticklish thing sinning against the Holy Ghost. "*It shall not be forgiven him.*"

Didn't I tell you there was Doom?

It shall not be forgiven her.

The Father forgives: the Son forgives: but the Holy Ghost does *not* forgive. So take that.

The Holy Ghost doesn't forgive because the Holy Ghost is within you. The Holy Ghost *is* you: your very You. So if, in your conceit of your ego, you make a break in your own YOU, in your own integrity, how can you be forgiven? You might as well make a rip in your own bowels. You *know* if you rip your own bowels they will go rotten and *you* will go rotten. And there's an end of you, in the body.

The same if you make a breach with your own Holy Ghost. You go soul-rotten. Like the Pearls.

These dear Pearls, they do anything they like, and remain pure. Oh, purity!

But they can't stop themselves from going rotten inside. Rotten Pearls, fair outside. Their *souls* smell, because their souls are putrefying inside them.

The sin against the Holy Ghost.

And gradually, from within outwards, they rot. Some form of dementia. A thing disintegrating. A decomposing psyche. Dementia.

Quos vult perdere Deus, dementat prius.

Watch these Pearls, these Pearls of modern women. Particularly American women. Battening on love. And fluttering in the first batlike throes of dementia.

You *can* have your cake and eat it. But my God, it will go rotten inside you.

Hawthorne's other books are nothing compared to *The Scarlet Letter*.

But there are good parables, and wonderful dark glimpses of early Puritan America, in *Twice Told Tales*.

The House of the Seven Gables has "atmosphere". The passing of the old order of the proud, bearded, black-browed Father: an order which is slowly ousted from life, and lingeringly haunts the old dark places. But comes a new generation to sweep out even the ghosts, with these new vacuum cleaners. No ghost could stand up against a vacuum cleaner.

The new generation is having no ghosts or cobwebs. It is setting up in the photography line, and is just going to make a sound financial thing out of it. For this purpose all old hates and old glooms, that belong to the antique order of Haughty Fathers, all these are swept up in the vacuum cleaner, and the vendetta-born young couple effect a perfect understanding under the black cloth of a camera and prosperity. *Vivat Industria!*

Oh, Nathaniel, you savage ironist! Ugh, how you'd have *hated* it if you'd had nothing but the prosperous, "dear" young couple to write about! If you'd lived to the day when America was nothing but a Main Street.

The Dark Old Fathers.

The Beloved Wishy-Washy Sons.

The Photography Business.

? ? ?

Hawthorne came nearest to actuality in the *Blithedale Romance*. This novel is a sort of picture of the notorious Brook Farm experiment. There the famous idealists and transcendentalists of America met to till the soil and hew the timber in the sweat of their own brows, thinking high thoughts the while, and breathing an atmosphere of communal love, and tingling in tune with the Oversoul, like so many strings of a super-celestial harp. An old twang of the Crèvecœur instrument.

Of course they fell out like cats and dogs. Couldn't stand one another. And all the music they made was the music of their quarrelling.

You *can't* idealize hard work. Which is why America invents so many machines and contrivances of all sort: so that they need do no physical work.

And that's why the idealists left off brookfarming, and took to bookfarming.

You *can't* idealize the essential brute blood-activity, the brute blood desires, the basic, sardonic blood-knowledge.

That you *can't* idealize.

And you can't eliminate it.

So there's the end of ideal man.

Man is made up of a dual consciousness, of which the two halves are most of the time in opposition to one another—and will be so as long as time lasts.

You've got to learn to change from one consciousness to the other, turn and about. Not to try to make either absolute, or dominant. The Holy Ghost tells you the how and when.

Never did Nathaniel feel himself more spectral—of course he went brookfarming—than when he was winding the horn in the morning to summon the transcendental labourers to their tasks, or than when marching off with a hoe ideally to hoe the turnips, "Never did I feel more spectral," says Nathaniel.

Never did I feel such a fool, would have been more to the point.

Farcical fools, trying to idealize labour. You'll never succeed in idealizing hard work. Before you can dig mother earth you've got to take off your ideal jacket. The harder a man works, at brute labour, the thinner becomes his idealism, the darker his mind. And the harder a man works, at mental labour, at idealism, at transcendental occupations, the thinner becomes his blood, and the more brittle his nerves.

Oh, the brittle-nerved brookfarmers!

You've got to be able to do both: the mental work, and the brute work. But be prepared to step from one pair of shoes into another. Don't try and make it all one pair of shoes.

The attempt to idealize the blood!

Nathaniel knew he was a fool, attempting it.

He went home to his amiable spouse and his sanctum sanctorum of a study.

Nathaniel!

But the *Blithedale Romance*. It has a beautiful, wintry-evening farm-kitchen sort of opening.

Dramatis Personæ :

1. *I.*—The narrator: whom we will call Nathaniel. A wisp of a sensitive, withal deep, literary young man no longer so very young.

2. *Zenobia :* a dark, proudly voluptuous clever woman with a tropical flower in her hair. Said to be sketched from Margaret Fuller, in whom Hawthorne saw some "evil nature". Nathaniel was more aware of Zenobia's voluptuousness than of her "mind".

3. *Hollingsworth :* a black-bearded blacksmith with a deep-voiced lust for saving criminals. Wants to build a great Home for these unfortunates.

4. *Priscilla :* a sort of White Lily, a clinging little mediumistic sempstress who has been made use of in public seances. A sort of prostitute soul.

5. *Zenobia's Husband :* an unpleasant decayed person with magnetic powers and teeth full of gold—or set in gold. It is he who has given public spiritualist demonstrations, with Priscilla for the medium. He is of the dark, sensual, decayed-handsome sort, and comes in unexpectedly by the back door.

Plot I.—I, Nathaniel, at once catch cold, and have to be put to bed. Am nursed with inordinate tenderness by the blacksmith, whose great hands are gentler than a woman's, etc.

The two men love one another with a love surpassing the love of women, so long as the healing-and-salvation business lasts. When Nathaniel wants to get well and have a soul of his own, he turns with hate to this black-bearded, booming salvationist, Hephæstos of the underworld. Hates him for tyrannous monomaniac.

Plot II.—Zenobia, that clever lustrous woman, is fascinated by the criminal-saving blacksmith, and would have him at any price. Meanwhile she has the subtlest current of understanding with the frail but deep Nathaniel. And she takes the White Lily half-pityingly, half contemptuously under a rich and glossy dark wing.

Plot III.—The blacksmith is after Zenobia, to get her money for his criminal asylum: of which, of course, he will be the first inmate.

Plot IV.—Nathaniel also feels his mouth watering for the dark-luscious Zenobia.

Plot V.—The White Lily, Priscilla, vaporously festering, turns out to be the famous Veiled Lady of public spiritualist shows: she whom the undesirable Husband, called the Professor, has used as a medium. Also she is Zenobia's half-sister.

Débâcle

Nobody wants Zenobia in the end. She goes off without her flower. The blacksmith marries Priscilla. Nathaniel dribblingly confesses that he, too, has loved Prissy all the while. Boo-hoo!

Conclusion

A few years after, Nathaniel meets the blacksmith in a country lane near a humble cottage, leaning totteringly on the arm of the frail but fervent Priscilla. Gone are all dreams of asylums, and the saviour of criminals can't even save himself from his own Veiled Lady.

There you have a nice little bunch of idealists, transcendentalists, brookfarmers, and disintegrated gentry. All going slightly rotten.

Two Pearls: a white Pearl and a black Pearl: the latter more expensive, lurid with money.

The white Pearl, the little medium, Priscilla, the imitation pearl, has truly some "supernormal" powers. She could drain the blacksmith of his blackness and his smith-strength.

Priscilla, the little psychic prostitute. The degenerate descendant of Ligeia. The absolutely yielding, "loving" woman, who abandons herself utterly to her lover. Or even to a gold-toothed "professor" of spiritualism.

Is it all bunkum, this spiritualism? Is it just rot, this Veiled Lady?

Not quite. Apart even from telepathy, the apparatus of human consciousness is the most wonderful message-receiver in existence. Beats a wireless station to nothing.

Put Prissy under the tablecloth then. Miaow!

What happens? Prissy under the tablecloth, like a canary when you cover his cage, goes into a "sleep", a trance.

A trance, not a sleep. A trance means that all her *individual*, personal intelligence goes to sleep, like a hen with her head under her wing. But the *apparatus* of consciousness remains working. Without a soul in it.

And what can this apparatus of consciousness do, when it works? Why, surely something. A wireless apparatus goes tick-tick-tick, taking down messages. So does your human apparatus. All kinds of messages. Only the soul, or the under-consciousness, deals with these messages in the dark, in the under-conscious. Which is the natural course of events.

But what sorts of messages? All sorts. Vibrations from the stars, vibrations from unknown magnetos, vibrations from unknown people, unknown passions. The human apparatus receives them all and they are all dealt with in the under-conscious.

There are also vibrations of thought, many, many. Necessary to get the two human instruments in key.

There may even be vibrations of ghosts in the air. Ghosts being dead *wills*, mind you, not dead souls. The soul has nothing to do with these dodges.

But some unit of force may persist for a time, after the death of an individual—some associations of vibrations may linger like little clouds in the etheric atmosphere after the death of a human being, or an animal. And these little clots of vibration may transfer themselves to the conscious-apparatus of the medium. So that the dead son of a disconsolate widow may send a message to his mourning mother to tell her that he owes Bill Jackson seven dollars: or that Uncle Sam's will is in the back of the bureau: and cheer up, Mother, I'm all right.

There is never much worth in these "messages", because they are never more than fragmentary items of dead, disintegrated consciousness. And the medium has, and always will have, a hopeless job, trying to disentangle the muddle of messages.

Again, coming events *may* cast their shadow before. The oracle may receive on her conscious-apparatus material vibrations to say that the next great war will break out in 1925. And in so far as the realm of cause-and-effect is master of the living soul, in so far as events are mechanically maturing, the forecast may be true.

But the living souls of men may upset the *mechanical* march of events at any moment.

Rien de certain.

Vibrations of subtlest matter. Concatenations of vibrations and shocks! Spiritualism.

And what then? It is all just materialistic, and a good deal is, and always will be, charlatanry.

Because the real human soul, the Holy Ghost, has its own deep prescience, which will not be put into figures, but flows on dark, a stream of prescience.

And the real human soul is too proud, and too sincere in its belief in the Holy Ghost that is within, to stoop to the practices of these spiritualist and other psychic tricks of material vibrations.

Because the first part of reverence is the acceptance of the fact that the Holy Ghost will never materialize: will never be anything but a ghost.

And the second part of reverence is the watchful observance of the motions, the comings and goings within us, of the Holy Ghost, and of the many gods that make up the Holy Ghost.

The Father had his day, and fell.

The Son has had his day, and fell.

It is the day of the Holy Ghost.

But when souls fall corrupt, into disintegration, they have no more day. They have sinned against the Holy Ghost.

These people in *Blithedale Romance* have sinned against the Holy Ghost, and corruption has set in.

All, perhaps, except the I, Nathaniel. He is still a sad, integral consciousness.

But not excepting Zenobia. The Black Pearl is rotting down. Fast. The cleverer she is, the faster she rots.

And they are all disintegrating, so they take to psychic

tricks. It is a certain sign of the disintegration of the psyche in a man, and much more so in a woman, when she takes to spiritualism, and table-rapping, and occult messages, or witchcraft and supernatural powers of that sort. When men want to be supernatural, be sure that something has gone wrong in their natural stuff. More so, even, with a woman.

And yet the soul has its own profound subtleties of knowing. And the blood has its strange omniscience.

But this isn't impudent and materialistic, like spiritualism and magic and all that range of pretentious supernaturalism.

CHAPTER IX

DANA'S "TWO YEARS BEFORE THE MAST"

You can't idealize brute labour. That is to say, you can't idealize brute labour, without coming undone, as an idealist.

The soil! The great ideal of the soil. Novels like Thomas Hardy's and pictures like the Frenchman Millet's. The soil.

What happens when you idealize the soil, the mother-earth, and really go back to it? Then with overwhelming conviction it is borne in upon you, as it was upon Thomas Hardy, that the whole scheme of things is against you. The whole massive rolling of natural fate is coming down on you like a slow glacier, to crush you to extinction. As an idealist.

Thomas Hardy's pessimism is an absolutely true finding. It is the absolutely true statement of the idealist's last realization, as he wrestles with the bitter soil of beloved mother-earth. He loves her, loves her, loves her. And she just entangles and crushes him like a slow Laocoön snake. The idealist must perish, says mother-earth. Then let him perish.

The great imaginative love of the soil itself! Tolstoi had it, and Thomas Hardy. And both are driven to a kind of fanatic denial of life, as a result.

You can't idealize mother-earth. You can try. You can even succeed. But succeeding, you succumb. She will have no pure idealist sons. None.

If you are a child of mother-earth, you must learn to discard your ideal self, in season, as you discard your clothes at night.

Americans have never loved the soil of America as Europeans have loved the soil of Europe. America has never been a blood-home-land. Only an ideal home-land. The home-land of the idea, of the *spirit*. And of the pocket. Not of the blood.

That has yet to come, when the idea and the spirit have collapsed from their false tyranny.

Europe has been loved with a blood love. That has made it beautiful.

In America, you have Fenimore Cooper's beautiful landscape: but that is wish-fulfilment, done from a distance. And you have Thoreau in Concord. But Thoreau sort of isolated his own bit of locality and put it under a lens, to examine it. He almost anatomized it, with his admiration.

America isn't a blood-home-land. For every American, the blood-home-land is Europe. The spirit-home-land is America.

Transcendentalism. Transcend this home-land business, exalt the idea of These States till you have made it a universal idea, says the true American. The oversoul is a world-soul, not a local thing.

So, in the next great move of imaginative conquest, Americans turned to the sea. Not to the land. Earth is too specific, too particular. Besides, the blood of white men is wine of no American soil. No, no.

But the blood of all men is ocean-born. We have our material universality, our blood-oneness, in the sea. The salt water.

You can't idealize the soil. But you've got to try. And trying, you reap a great imaginative reward. And the greatest reward is failure. To know you have failed, that you *must* fail. That is the greatest comfort of all, at last.

Tolstoi failed with the soil: Thomas Hardy too: and Giovanni Verga; the three greatest.

The further extreme, the greatest mother, is the sea. Love the great mother of the sea, the Magna Mater. And see how bitter it is. And see how you must fail to win her to your ideal: forever fail. Absolutely fail.

Swinburne tried in England. But the Americans made the greatest trial. The most vivid failure.

At a certain point, human life becomes uninteresting to men. What then? They turn to some universal.

The greatest material mother of us all is the sea.

Dana's eyes failed him when he was studying at Harvard. And suddenly, he turned to the sea, the naked Mother. He went to sea as a common sailor before the mast.

You can't idealize brute labour. Yet you can. You can

go through with brute labour, and *know* what it means. You can even meet and match the sea, and KNOW her.

This is what Dana wanted: a naked fighting experience with the sea.

KNOW THYSELF. That means, know the earth that is in your blood. Know the sea that is in your blood. The great elementals.

But we must repeat: KNOWING and BEING are opposite, antagonistic states. The more you know, exactly, the less you *are*. The more you *are*, in being, the less you know.

This is the great cross of man, his dualism. The blood-self, and the nerve-brain self.

Knowing, then, is the slow death of being. Man has his epochs of being, his epochs of knowing. It will always be a great oscillation. The goal is to know how not-to-know.

Dana took another great step in knowing: knowing the mother sea. But it was a step also in his own undoing. It was a new phase of dissolution of his own being. Afterwards, he would be a less human thing. He would be a knower: but more near to mechanism than before. That is our cross, our doom.

And so he writes, in his first days at sea, in winter, on the Atlantic: "Nothing will compare with the *early breaking of the day* upon the wide ocean. There is something in the first grey streaks stretching along the eastern horizon, and throwing an indistinct light upon the face of the deep, which creates . . . a feeling of loneliness, of dread, and of melancholy foreboding, which nothing else in nature can give."

So he ventures wakeful and alone into the great naked watery universe of the end of life, the twilight place where integral being lapses, and warm life begins to give out. It is man moving on into the face of death, the great adventure, the great undoing, the strange extension of the consciousness. The same in his vision of the albatross. "But one of the finest sights that I have ever seen was an albatross asleep upon the water, during a calm off Cape Horn, when a heavy sea was running. There being no breeze, the surface of the water was unbroken, but a long, heavy swell was rolling, and we saw the fellow, all white, directly ahead of us, asleep upon the waves, with his head under his wing; now rising on the top of a huge billow, and then falling slowly until he was lost in the hollow between. He was undisturbed for some time, until the noise of our bows, gradually approaching, roused him, when, lifting his head, he stared upon us for a moment, and then spread his wide wings, and took his flight."

We must give Dana credit for a profound mystic vision. The best Americans are mystics by instinct. Simple and bare as his narrative is, it is deep with profound emotion and stark comprehension. He sees the last light-loving incarnation of life exposed upon the eternal waters: a speck, solitary upon the verge of the two naked principles, aerial and watery. And his own soul is as the soul of the albatross.

It is a storm-bird. And so is Dana. He has gone down to fight with the sea. It is a metaphysical, actual struggle of an integral soul with the vast, non-living, yet potent element. Dana never forgets, never ceases to watch. If Hawthorne was a spectre on the land, how much more is Dana a spectre at sea. But he must watch, he must know, he must conquer the sea in his consciousness. This is the poignant difference between him and the common sailor. The common sailor lapses from consciousness, becomes elemental like a seal, a creature. Tiny and alone, Dana watches the great seas mount round his own small body. If he is swept away, some other man will have to take up what he has begun. For the sea must be mastered by the human consciousness, in the great fight of the human soul for mastery over life and death, in KNOWLEDGE. It is the last bitter necessity of the Tree. The Cross. Impartial, Dana beholds himself among the elements, calm and fatal. His style is great and hopeless, the style of a perfect tragic recorder.

"Between five and six the cry of 'All starbowlines ahoy!' summoned our watch on deck, and immediately all hands were called. A great cloud of a dark slate-colour was driving on us from the south-west; and we did our best to take in sail before we were in the midst of it. We had got the light-sails furled, the courses hauled up, and the topsail reef-tackles hauled out, and were just mounting the forerigging when the storm struck us. In an instant the sea, which had been comparatively quiet, was running higher and higher; and it became almost as dark as night. The hail and sleet were harder than I had yet felt them, seeming almost to pin us down to the rigging."

It is in the dispassionate statement of plain material facts that Dana achieves his greatness. Dana writes from the remoter, non-emotional centres of being—not from the passional emotional self.

So the ship battles on, round Cape Horn, then into quieter seas. The island of Juan Fernandez, Crusoe's island, rises like a dream from the sea, like a green cloud, and like a ghost Dana watches it, feeling only a faint, ghostly pang of regret for the life that was.

But the strain of the long sea-voyage begins to tell. The sea is a great disintegrative force. Its tonic quality is its disintegrative quality. It burns down the tissue, liberates energy. And after a long time, this burning-down is destructive. The psyche becomes destroyed, irritable, frayed, almost dehumanized.

So there is trouble on board the ship, irritating discontent, friction unbearable, and at last a flogging. This flogging rouses Dana for the first and last time to human and ideal passion.

"Sam by this time was seized up—that is, placed against the shrouds, with his wrists made fast to the shrouds, his jacket off, and his back exposed. The captain stood on the break of the deck, a few feet from him, and a little raised, so as to have a good swing at him, and held in his hand the bight of a thick, strong rope. The officers stood round, and the crew grouped together in the waist. All these preparations made me feel sick and almost faint, angry and excited as I was. A man—a human being made in God's likeness—fastened up and flogged like a beast! The first and almost uncontrollable impulse was resistance. But what was to be done?—The time for it had gone by——"

So Mr. Dana couldn't act. He could only lean over the side of the ship and spew.

Whatever made him vomit?

Why shall man not be whipped?

As long as man has a bottom, he must surely be whipped. It is as if the Lord intended it so.

Why? For lots of reasons.

Man doth not live by bread alone, to absorb it and to evacuate it.

What is the breath of life? My dear, it is the strange current of interchange that flows between men and men, and men and women, and men and things. A constant current of interflow, a constant vibrating interchange. That is the breath of life.

And this interflow, this electric vibration is polarized. There is a positive and a negative polarity. This is a law of life, of vitalism.

Only ideas are final, finite, static, and single.

All life-interchange is a polarized communication. A circuit.

There are lots of circuits. Male and female, for example, and master and servant. The idea, the IDEA, that fixed gorgon monster, and the IDEAL, that great stationary engine, these two gods-of-the-machine have been busy destroying all *natural* reciprocity and *natural* circuits, for centuries. IDEAS have played the very old Harry with sex relationship, that is, with the great circuit of man and woman. Turned the thing into a wheel on which the human being in both is broken. And the IDEAL has mangled the blood-reciprocity of master and servant into an abstract horror.

Master and servant—or master and man relationship is, essentially, a polarized flow, like love. It is a circuit of vitalism which flows between master and man and forms a very precious nourishment to each, and keeps both in a state of subtle, quivering, vital equilibrium. Deny it as you like, it is so. But once you *abstract* both master and man, and make them both serve an *idea*: production, wage, efficiency, and so on: so that each looks on himself as an instrument performing a certain repeated evolution, then you have changed the vital, quivering circuit of master and man into a mechanical machine unison. Just another way of life: or anti-life.

You could never quite do this on a sailing ship. A master had to be master, or it was hell. That is, there had to be this strange interflow of master-and-man, the strange reciprocity of command and obedience.

The reciprocity of command and obedience is a state of unstable vital equilibrium. Everything vital, or natural, is unstable, thank God.

The ship had been at sea many weeks. A great strain on master and men. An increasing callous indifference in the men, an increasing irritability in the master.

And then what?

A storm.

Don't expect me to say *why* storms must be. They just are. Storms in the air, storms in the water, storms of thunder, storms of anger. Storms just are.

Storms are a sort of violent readjustment in some polarized flow. You have a polarized circuit, a circuit of unstable equilibrium. The instability increases till there is a crash. Everything seems to break down. Thunder roars, lightning flashes. The master roars, the whip whizzes. The sky sends down sweet rain. The ship knows a new strange stillness, a readjustment, a refinding of equilibrium.

Ask the Lord Almighty why it is so. I don't know. I know it is so.

But flogging? Why flogging? Why not use reason or take away jam for tea?

Why not? Why not ask the thunder please to abstain from this physical violence of crashing and thumping, please to swale away like thawing snow.

Sometimes the thunder *does* swale away like thawing snow, and then you hate it. Muggy, sluggish, inert, dreary sky.

Flogging.

You have a Sam, a fat slow fellow, who has got slower and more slovenly as the weeks wear on. You have a master who has grown more irritable in his authority. Till Sam becomes simply wallowing in his slackness, makes your gorge rise. And the master is on red hot iron.

Now these two men, Captain and Sam, are there in a very unsteady equilibrium of command and obedience. A polarized flow. Definitely polarized.

The poles of will are the great ganglia of the voluntary nerve system, located beside the spinal column, in the back. From the poles of will in the backbone of the Captain, to the ganglia of will in the back of the sloucher Sam, runs a frazzled, jagged current, a staggering circuit of vital electricity. This circuit gets one jolt too many, and there is an explosion.

"Tie up that lousy swine!" roars the enraged Captain.

And whack! whack! down on the bare back of that sloucher Sam comes the cat.

What does it do? By Jove, it goes like ice-cold water into his spine. Down those lashes runs the current of the

Captain's rage, right into the blood and into the toneless ganglia of Sam's voluntary system. Crash! Crash! runs the lightning flame, right into the cores of the living nerves.

And the living nerves respond. They start to vibrate. They brace up. The blood begins to go quicker. The nerves begin to recover their vividness. It is their tonic. The man Sam has a new clear day of intelligence, and a smarty back. The Captain has a new relief, a new ease in his authority, and a sore heart.

There is a new equilibrium, and a fresh start. The *physical* intelligence of a Sam is restored, the turgidity is relieved from the veins of the Captain.

It is a natural form of human coition, interchange.

It is good for Sam to be flogged. It is good, on this occasion, for the Captain to have Sam flogged. I say so. Because they were both in that physical condition.

Spare the rod and spoil the *physical* child.

Use the rod and spoil the *ideal* child.

There you are.

Dana, as an idealist, refusing the blood-contact of life, leaned over the side of the ship powerless, and vomited: or wanted to. His solar plexus was getting a bit of its own back. To him, Sam was an "ideal" being, who should have been approached through the mind, the reason, and the spirit. That lump of a Sam!

But there was another idealist on board, the seaman John, a Swede. He wasn't named John for nothing, this Jack-tar of the Logos. John felt himself called upon to play Mediator, Interceder, Saviour, on this occasion. The popular Paraclete.

"Why are you whipping this man, sir?"

But the Captain had got his dander up. He wasn't going to have his natural passion judged and interfered with by these long-nosed salvationist Johannuses. So he had nosey John hauled up and whipped as well.

For which I am very glad.

Alas, however, the Captain got the worst of it in the end. He smirks longest who smirks last. The Captain wasn't wary enough. Natural anger, natural passion has its unremitting enemy in the idealist. And the ship was already tainted with idealism. A good deal more so, apparently, than Herman Melville's ships were.

Which reminds us that Melville was once going to be flogged. In *White Jacket*. And he, too, would have taken it as the last insult.

In my opinion there are worse insults than floggings. I would rather be flogged than have most people "like" me.

Melville too had an Interceder: a quiet, self-respecting man, not a saviour. The man spoke in the name of Justice. Melville was to be unjustly whipped. The man spoke honestly and quietly. Not in any salvationist spirit. And the whipping did not take place.

Justice is a great and manly thing. Saviourism is a despicable thing.

Sam was justly whipped. It was a passional justice.

But Melville's whipping would have been a cold, disciplinary injustice. A foul thing. Mechanical *justice* even is a foul thing. For true justice makes the heart's fibres quiver. You can't be cold in a matter of real justice.

Already in those days it was no fun to be a captain. You had to learn already to abstract yourself into a machine-part, exerting machine-control. And it is a good deal bitterer to exert machine-control, selfless, ideal control, than it is to have to obey, mechanically. Because the idealists who mechanically obey almost always hate the *man* who must give the orders. Their idealism rarely allows them to exonerate the man for the office.

Dana's captain was one of the real old-fashioned sort. He gave himself away terribly. He should have been more wary, knowing he confronted a shipful of enemies and at least two cold and deadly idealists, who hated all "masters" on principle.

"As he went on, his passion increased, and he danced about the deck, calling out as he swung the rope, 'If you want to know what I flog you for, I'll tell you. It's because I like to do it!—Because I like to do it!—It suits me. That's what I do it for!'

"The man writhed under the pain. My blood ran cold, I could look on no longer. Disgusted, sick and horror-stricken, I turned away and leaned over the rail and looked down in the water. A few rapid thoughts of my own situation, and of the prospect of future revenge, crossed my mind; but the falling of the blows, and the cries of the man called me back at once. At length they ceased, and, turning round, I found that the Mate, at a signal from the captain, had cut him down."

After all, it was not so terrible. The captain evidently did not exceed the ordinary measure. Sam got no more than he asked for. It was a natural event. All would have been well, save for the *moral* verdict. And this came from theoretic idealists like Dana and the seaman John, rather than from the sailors themselves. The sailors understood spontaneous *passional* morality, not the artificial ethical. They respected the violent readjustments of the naked force, in man as in nature.

"The flogging was seldom, if ever, alluded to by us in the forecastle. If any one was inclined to talk about it, the others, with a delicacy which I hardly expected to find among them, always stopped him, or turned the subject."

Two men had been flogged: the second and the elder, John, for interfering and asking the captain why he flogged Sam. It is while flogging John that the captain shouts, "If you want to know what I flog you for, I'll tell you——"

"But the behaviour of the two men who were flogged," Dana continues, "toward one another, showed a delicacy and a sense of honour which would have been worthy of admiration in the highest walks of life. Sam knew that the other had suffered solely on his account, and in all his complaints he said that if he alone had been flogged it would have been nothing, but that he never could see that man without thinking what had been the means of bringing that disgrace upon him; and John never, by word or deed, let anything escape him to remind the other that it was by interfering to save his shipmate that he had suffered."

As a matter of fact, it was John who ought to have been ashamed for bringing confusion and false feeling into a clear issue. Conventional morality apart, John is the reprehensible party, not Sam or the captain. The case was one of passional readjustment, nothing abnormal. And who was the sententious Johannus, that he should interfere in this? And if Mr. Dana had a weak stomach as well as weak eyes, let him have it. But let this pair of idealists abstain from making all the other men feel uncomfortable and fuzzy about a thing they would have left to its natural course, if they had been allowed. No, your Johannuses and your

Danas have to be creating "public opinion", and mugging up the life-issues with their sententiousness. O idealism!

The vessel arrives at the Pacific coast, and the swell of the rollers falls in our blood—the weary coast stretches wonderful, on the brink of the unknown.

"Not a human being but ourselves for miles—the steep hill rising like a wall, and cutting us off from all the world —but the 'world of waters'. I separated myself from the rest, and sat down on a rock, just where the sea ran in and formed a fine spouting-horn. Compared with the dull, plain sand-beach of the rest of the coast, this grandeur was as refreshing as a great rock in a weary land. It was almost the first time I had been positively alone. . . . My better nature returned strong upon me. I experienced a glow of pleasure at finding that what of poetry and romance I had ever had in me had not been entirely deadened in the laborious life I had been lately leading. Nearly an hour did I sit, almost lost in the luxury of this entire new scene of the play in which I was acting, when I was aroused by the distant shouts of my companions."

So Dana sits and Hamletizes by the Pacific—chief actor in the play of his own existence. But in him, self-consciousness is almost nearing the mark of scientific indifference to self.

He gives us a pretty picture of the then wild, unknown bay of San Francisco.—"The tide leaving us, we came to anchor near the mouth of the bay, under a high and beautifully sloping hill, upon which herds of hundreds of red deer and the stag with his high-branching antlers were bounding about, looking at us for a moment, and then starting off affrighted at the noises we made for the purpose of seeing the variety of their beautiful attitudes and motions——"

Think of it now, and the Presidio! The idiotic guns.

Two moments of strong human emotion Dana experiences: one moment of strong but impotent hate for the captain, one strong impulse of pitying love for the Kanaka boy, Hope—a beautiful South Sea Islander sick of a white man's disease, phthisis or syphilis. Of him Dana writes— "but the other, who was my friend, and Aikane—Hope— was the most dreadful object I had ever seen in my life; his hands looking like claws; a dreadful cough, which seemed to rack his whole shattered system; a hollow, whispering voice, and an entire inability to move himself. There he lay, upon a mat on the ground, which was the only floor of the oven, with no medicine, no comforts, and no one to care for or help him but a few Kanakas, who were willing enough, but could do nothing. The sight of him made me sick and faint. Poor fellow! During the four months that I lived upon the beach we were continually together, both in work and in our excursions in the woods and upon the water. I really felt a strong affection for him, and preferred him to any of my own countrymen there. When I came into the oven he looked at me, held out his hand and said in a low voice, but with a delightful smile, 'Aloha, Aikane! Aloha nui!' I comforted him as well as I could, and promised to ask the captain to help him from the medicine chest."

We have felt the pulse of hate for the captain—now the pulse of Saviour-like love for the bright-eyed man of the Pacific, a real child of the ocean, full of the mystery-being of that great sea. Hope is for a moment to Dana what Chingachgook is to Cooper—the heart's-brother, the answerer. But only for an ephemeral moment. And even then his love was largely pity, tinged with philanthropy. The inevitable saviourism. The ideal being.

Dana was mad to leave the California coast, to be back in the civilized east. Yet he feels the poignancy of departure when at last the ship draws off. The Pacific is his glamour-world: the eastern States his world of actuality, scientific, materially real. He is a servant of civilization, an idealist, a democrat, a hater of masters, a KNOWER. Conscious and self-conscious, without ever forgetting.

"When all sail had been set and the decks cleared up, the *California* was a speck in the horizon, and the coast lay like a low cloud along the north-east. At sunset they were both out of sight, and we were once more upon the ocean, where sky and water meet."

The description of the voyage home is wonderful. It is as if the sea rose up to prevent the escape of this subtle explorer. Dana seems to pass into another world, another life, not of this earth. There is first the sense of apprehension, then the passing right into the black deeps. Then the waters almost swallow him up, with his triumphant consciousness.

"The days became shorter and shorter, the sun running lower in its course each day, and giving less and less heat, and the nights so cold as to prevent our sleeping on deck; the Magellan Clouds in sight of a clear night; the skies looking cold and angry; and at times a long, heavy, ugly sea, setting in from the Southward, told us what we were coming to."

They were approaching Cape Horn, in the southern winter, passing into the strange, dread regions of the violent waters.

"And there lay, floating in the ocean, several miles off, an immense irregular mass, its top and points covered with snow, its centre a deep indigo. This was an iceberg, and of the largest size. As far as the eye could reach, the sea in every direction was of a deep blue colour, the waves running high and fresh, and sparkling in the light; and in the midst lay this immense mountain-island, its cavities and valleys thrown into deep shade, and its points and pinnacles glittering in the sun. But no description can give any idea of the strangeness, splendour, and, really, the sublimity of the sight. Its great size—for it must have been two or three miles in circumference, and several hundred feet in height; its slow motion, as its base rose and sank in the water and its points nodded against the clouds; the high dashing of the waves upon it, which, breaking high with foam, lined its base with a white crust; and the thundering sound of the cracking of the mass, and the breaking and tumbling down of huge pieces; together with its nearness and approach, which added a slight element of fear—all combined to give it the character of true sublimity——"

But as the ship ran further and further into trouble, Dana became ill. First it is a slight toothache. Ice and exposure cause the pains to take hold of all his head and face. And then the face so swelled, that he could not open his mouth to eat, and was in danger of lock-jaw. In this state he was forced to keep his bunk for three or four days. "At the end of the third day, the ice was very thick; a complete fog-bank covered the ship. It blew a tremendous gale from the eastward, with sleet and snow, and there was every promise of a dangerous and fatiguing night. At dark, the captain called the hands aft, and told them that not a man was to leave the deck that night; that the ship was in the greatest danger; any cake of ice might knock a hole in her, or she might run on an island and go to pieces. The look-outs were then set, and every man was put in his station. When I heard what was the state of things, I began to put on my things, to stand it out with the rest of them, when the mate came below, and looking at my face ordered me back to my berth, saying if we went down we should all go down together, but if I went on deck I might lay myself up for life. In obedience to the mate's orders, I went back to my berth; but a more miserable night I never wish to spend."

It is the story of a man pitted in conflict against the sea, the vast, almost omnipotent element. In contest with this cosmic enemy, man finds his further ratification, his further ideal vindication. He comes out victorious, but not till the sea has tortured his living, integral body, and made him pay something for his triumph in consciousness.

The horrific struggle round Cape Horn, homewards, is the crisis of the Dana history. It is an entry into chaos, a heaven of sleet and black ice-rain, a sea of ice and iron-like water. Man fights the element in all its roused, mystic hostility to conscious life. This fight is the inward crisis and triumph of Dana's soul. He goes through it all consciously, enduring, *knowing*. It is not a mere overcoming of obstacles. It is a pitting of the deliberate consciousness against all the roused, hostile, anti-life waters of the Pole.

After this fight, Dana has achieved his success. He knows. He knows what the sea is. He knows what the Cape Horn is. He knows what work is, work before the mast. He knows, he knows a great deal. He has carried his consciousness open-eyed through it all. He has won through. The ideal being.

And from his book, we know too. He has lived this great experience for us; we owe him homage.

The ship passes through the strait, strikes the polar death-mystery, and turns northward, home. She seems to fly with new strong plumage, free. "Every rope-yarn seemed stretched to the utmost, and every thread of the canvas; and with this sail added to her the ship sprang through the water like a thing possessed. The sail being nearly all forward, it lifted her out of the water, and she seemed actually to jump from sea to sea."

Beautifully the sailing-ship nodalizes the forces of sea

and wind, converting them to her purpose. There is no violation, as in a steam-ship, only a winged centrality. It is this perfect adjusting of ourselves to the elements, the perfect equipoise between them and us, which gives us a great part of our life-joy. The more we intervene machinery between us and the naked forces the more we numb and atrophy our own senses. Every time we turn on a tap to have water, every time we turn a handle to have fire or light, we deny ourselves and annul our being. The great elements, the earth, air, fire, water, are there like some great mistress whom we woo and struggle with, whom we heave and wrestle with. And all our appliances do but deny us these fine embraces, take the miracle of life away from us. The machine is the great neuter. It is the eunuch of eunuchs. In the end it emasculates us all. When we balance the sticks and kindle a fire, we partake of the mysteries. But when we turn on an electric tap there is, as it were, a wad between us and the dynamic universe. We do not know what we lose by all our labour-saving appliances. Of the two evils it would be much the lesser to lose all machinery, every bit, rather than to have, as we have, hopelessly too much.

When we study the pagan gods, we find they have now one meaning, now another. Now they belong to the creative essence, and now to the material-dynamic world. First they have one aspect, then another. The greatest god has both aspects. First he is the source of life. Then he is mystic dynamic lord of the elemental physical forces. So Zeus is Father, and Thunderer.

Nations that worship the material-dynamic world, as all nations do in their decadence, seem to come inevitably to worship the Thunderer. He is Ammon, Zeus, Wotan and Thor, Shango of the West Africans. As the creator of man himself, the Father is greatest in the creative world, the Thunderer is greatest in the material world. He is the god of force and of earthly blessing, the god of the bolt and of sweet rain.

So that electricity seems to be the first, intrinsic principle among the Forces. It has a mystic power of readjustment. It seems to be the overlord of the two naked elements, fire and water, capable of mysteriously enchaining them, and of mysteriously sundering them from their connexions.

When the two great elements become hopelessly clogged, entangled, the sword of the lightning can separate them. The crash of thunder is really not the clapping together of waves of air. Thunder is the noise of the explosion which takes place when the waters are loosed from the elemental fire, when old vapours are suddenly decomposed in the upper air by the electric force. Then fire flies fluid, and the waters roll off in purity. It is the liberation of the elements from hopeless conjunction. Thunder, the electric force, is the counterpart in the material-dynamic world of the life-force, the creative mystery, itself, in the creative world.

Dana gives a wonderful description of a tropical thunderstorm.

"When our watch came on deck at twelve o'clock it was as black as Erebus; not a breath was stirring; the sails hung heavy and motionless from the yards; and the perfect stillness, and the darkness, which was almost palpable, were truly appalling. Not a word was spoken, but everyone stood as though waiting for something to happen. In a few minutes the mate came forward, and in a low tone which was almost a whisper, gave the command to haul down the jib. When we got down we found all hands looking aloft, and then, directly over where we had been standing, upon the main top-gallant mast-head, was a ball of light, which the sailors name a corposant (*corpus sancti*). They were all watching it carefully, for sailors have a notion that if the corposant rises in the rigging, it is a sign of fair weather; but if it comes lower down, there will be a storm. Unfortunately, as an omen, it came down and showed itself on the top-gallant yard-arm.

"In a few minutes it disappeared and showed itself again on the fore top-gallant yard, and, after playing about for some time, disappeared again, when the man on the forecastle pointed to it upon the flying-jib-boom-end. But our attention was drawn from watching this by the falling of some drops of rain. In a few minutes low growling thunder was heard, and some random flashes of lightning came from the south-west. Every sail was taken in but the top-sail. A few puffs lifted the top-sails, but they fell again to the mast, and all was as still as ever. A minute more, and a terrific flash and peal broke simultaneously upon us, and a cloud appeared to open directly over our heads and let down the water in one body like a falling ocean. We stood motionless and almost stupefied, yet nothing had been struck. Peal after peal rattled over our heads with a sound which actually seemed to stop the breath in the body. The violent fall of the rain lasted but a few minutes, and was succeeded by occasional drops and showers; but the lightning continued incessant for several hours, breaking the midnight darkness with irregular and blinding flashes.

"During all this time hardly a word was spoken, no bell was struck, and the wheel was silently relieved. The rain fell at intervals in heavy showers, and we stood drenched through, and blinded by the flashes, which broke the Egyptian darkness with a brightness which seemed almost malignant, while the thunder rolled in peals, the concussion of which appeared to shake the very ocean. A ship is not often injured by lightning, for the electricity is separated by the great number of points she presents, and the quality of iron which she has scattered in various parts. The electric fluid ran over our anchors, topsail-sheets and ties; yet no harm was done to us. We went below at four o'clock, leaving things in the same state."

Dana is wonderful at relating these mechanical, or dynamic-physical events. He could not tell about the being of men: only about the forces. He gives another curious instance of the process of recreation, as it takes place within the very corpuscles of the blood. It is *salt* this time which arrests the life-activity, causing a static arrest in Matter, after a certain sundering of water from the fire of the warm-substantial body.

"The scurvy had begun to show itself on board. One man had it so badly as to be disabled and off duty; and the English lad, Ben, was in a dreadful state, and was gradually growing worse. His legs swelled and pained him so that he could not walk; his flesh lost its elasticity, so that if it were pressed in, it would not return to its shape; and his gums swelled until he could not open his mouth. His breath, too, became very offensive; he lost all strength and spirit; could eat nothing; grew worse every day; and, in fact, unless something was done for him, would be a dead man in a week at the rate at which he was sinking. The medicines were all gone, or nearly all gone; and if we had had a chest-full, they would have been of no use; for nothing but fresh provisions and terra firma has any effect upon the scurvy."

However, a boat-load of potatoes and onions was obtained from a passing ship. These the men ate raw.

"The freshness and crispness of the raw onion, with the earthy state, give it a great relish to one who has been a long time on salt provisions. We were perfectly ravenous after them. We ate them at every meal, by the dozen; and filled our pockets with them, to eat on the watch on deck. The chief use, however, of the fresh provisions was for the men with the scurvy. One was able to eat, and he soon brought himself to by gnawing upon raw potatoes; but the other, by this time, was hardly able to open his mouth; and the cook took the potatoes raw, pounded them in a mortar, and gave him the juice to suck. The strong earthy taste and smell of this extract of the raw potatoes at first produced a shuddering through his whole frame, and after drinking it, an acute pain, which ran through all parts of his body; but knowing by this that it was taking strong hold, he persevered, drinking a spoonful every hour or so, until, by the effect of this drink, and of his own restored hope, he became so well as to be able to move about, and open his mouth enough to eat the raw potatoes and onions pounded into a soft pulp. This course soon restored his appetite and strength; and ten days after we spoke the *Solon*, so rapid was his recovery that, from lying helpless and almost hopeless in his berth, he was at the mast-head, furling a royal."

This is the strange result of the disintegrating effect of the sea, and of salt food. We are all sea-born, science tells us. The moon, and the sea, and salt, and phosphorus, and us: it is a long chain of connexion. And then the earth: mother-earth. Dana talks of the relish which the *earthy* taste of the onion gives. The taste of created juice, the living milk of Gea. And limes, which taste of the sun.

How much stranger is the interplay of *life* among the elements, than any chemical interplay among the elements themselves. Life—and salt—and phosphorus—and the sea—and the moon. Life—and sulphur—and carbon—and volcanoes—and the sun. The way up, and the way down. The strange ways of life.

But Dana went home, to be a lawyer, and a rather dull and distinguished citizen. He was once almost an ambassador. And pre-eminently respectable.

He had been. He KNEW. He had even told us. It is a great achievement.

And then what?—Why, nothing. The old vulgar humdrum. That's the worst of knowledge. It leaves one only the more lifeless. Dana lived his bit in two years, and knew, and drummed out the rest. Dreary lawyer's years, afterwards.

We know enough, We know too much. We know nothing.

Let us smash something. Ourselves included. But the machine above all.

Dana's small book is a very great book: contains a great extreme of knowledge, knowledge of the great element.

And after all, we have to know all before we can know that knowing is nothing.

Imaginatively, we have to know all: even the elemental waters. And know and know on, until knowledge suddenly shrivels and we know that forever we don't know.

Then there is a sort of peace, and we can start afresh, knowing we don't know.

CHAPTER X

HERMAN MELVILLE'S "TYPEE" AND "OMOO"

THE greatest seer and poet of the sea for me is Melville. His vision is more real than Swinburne's, because he doesn't personify the sea, and far sounder than Joseph Conrad's, because Melville doesn't sentimentalize the ocean and the sea's unfortunates. Snivel in a wet hanky like Lord Jim.

Melville has the strange, uncanny magic of sea-creatures, and some of their repulsiveness. He isn't quite a land animal. There is something slithery about him. Something always half-seas-over. In his life they said he was mad—or crazy. He was neither mad nor crazy. But he was over the border. He was half a water animal, like those terrible yellow-bearded Vikings who broke out of the waves in beaked ships.

He was a modern Viking. There is something curious about real blue-eyed people. They are never quite human, in the good classic sense, human as brown-eyed people are human: the human of the living humus. About a real blue-eyed person there is usually something abstract, elemental. Brown-eyed people are, as it were, like the earth, which is tissue of bygone life, organic, compound. In blue eyes there is sun and rain and abstract, uncreate element, water, ice, air, space, but not humanity. Brown-eyed people are people of the old, old world: *Allzu menschlich*. Blue-eyed people tend to be too keen and abstract.

Melville is like a Viking going home to the sea, encumbered with age and memories, and a sort of accomplished despair, almost madness. For he cannot accept humanity. He can't belong to humanity. Cannot.

The great Northern cycle of which he is the returning unit has almost completed its round, accomplished itself. Balder the beautiful is mystically dead, and by this time he stinketh. Forget-me-nots and sea-poppies fall into water. The man who came from the sea to live among men can stand it no longer. He hears the horror of the cracked church bell, and goes back down the shore, back into the ocean again, home, into the salt water. Human life won't do. He turns back to the elements. And all the vast sun-and-wheat consciousness of his day he plunges back into the deeps, burying the flame in the deep, self-conscious and deliberate. As blue flax and sea-poppies fall into the waters and give back their created sun-stuff to the dissolution of the flood.

The sea-born people, who can meet and mingle no longer: who turn away from life, to the abstract, to the elements: the sea receives her own.

Let life come asunder, they say. Let water conceive no more with fire. Let mating finish. Let the elements leave off kissing, and turn their backs on one another. Let the merman turn away from his human wife and children, let the seal-woman forget the world of men, remembering only the waters.

So they go down to the sea, the sea-born people. The Vikings are wandering again. Homes are broken up. Cross the seas, cross the seas, urges the heart. Leave love and home. Leave love and home. Love and home are a deadly illusion. Woman, what have I to do with thee? It is finished. *Consummatum est*. The crucifixion into humanity is over. Let us go back to the fierce, uncanny elements: the corrosive vast sea. Or Fire.

Basta! It is enough. It is enough of life. Let us have the vast elements. Let us get out of this loathsome complication of living humanly with humans. Let the sea wash us clean of the leprosy of our humanity and humanness.

Melville was a northerner, sea-born. So the sea claimed him. We are most of us, who use the English language, water-people, sea-derived.

Melville went back to the oldest of all the oceans, to the Pacific. *Der Grosse oder Stille Ozean.*

Without doubt the Pacific Ocean is æons older than the Atlantic or the Indian Oceans. When we say older, we mean it has not come to any modern consciousness. Strange convulsions have convulsed the Atlantic and Mediterranean peoples into phase after phase of consciousness, while the Pacific and the Pacific peoples have slept. To sleep is to dream: you can't stay unconscious. And, oh heaven, for how many thousands of years has the true Pacific been dreaming, turning over in its sleep and dreaming again: idylls: nightmares.

The Maoris, the Tongans, the Marquesans, the Fijians, the Polynesians: holy God, how long have they been turning over in the same sleep, with varying dreams? Perhaps, to a sensitive imagination, those islands in the middle of the Pacific are the most unbearable places on earth. It simply stops the heart, to be translated there, unknown ages back, back into that life, that pulse, that rhythm. The scientists say the South Sea Islanders belong to the Stone Age. It seems absurd to class people according to their implements. And yet there is something in it. The heart of the Pacific is still the Stone Age; in spite of steamers. The heart of the Pacific seems like a vast vacuum, in which, mirage-like, continues the life of myriads of ages back. It is a phantom-persistence of human beings who should have died, by our chronology, in the Stone Age. It is a phantom, illusion-like trick of reality: the glamorous South Seas.

Even Japan and China have been turning over in their sleep for countless centuries. Their blood is the old blood, their tissue the old soft tissue. Their busy day was myriads of years ago, when the world was a softer place, more moisture in the air, more warm mud on the face of the earth, and the lotus was always in flower. The great bygone world, before Egypt. And Japan and China have been turning over in their sleep, while we have "advanced". And now they are starting up into nightmare.

The world isn't what it seems.

The Pacific Ocean holds the dream of immemorial centuries. It is the great blue twilight of the vastest of all evenings: perhaps of the most wonderful of all dawns. Who knows?

It must once have been a vast basin of soft, lotus-warm civilization, the Pacific. Never was such a huge man-day swung down into slow disintegration, as here. And now the waters are blue and ghostly with the end of immemorial peoples. And phantom-like the islands rise out of it, illusions of the glamorous Stone Age.

To this phantom Melville returned. Back, back, away from life. Never man instinctively hated human life, our human life, as we have it, more than Melville did. And never was a man so passionately filled with the sense of vastness and mystery of life which is non-human. He was mad to look over our horizons. Anywhere, anywhere out of *our* world. To get away. To get away, out!

To get away, out of our life. To cross a horizon into another life. No matter what life, so long as it is another life.

Away, away from humanity. To the sea. The naked salt, elemental sea. To go to sea, to escape humanity.

The human heart gets into a frenzy at last, in its desire to dehumanize itself.

So he finds himself in the middle of the Pacific. Truly over a horizon. In another world. In another epoch. Back, far back, in the days of palm trees and lizards and stone implements. The sunny Stone Age.

Samoa, Tahiti, Raratonga, Nukuheva: the very names are a sleep and a forgetting. The sleep-forgotten past magnificence of human history. "Trailing clouds of glory."

Melville hated the world: was born hating it. But he was looking for heaven. That is, choosingly. Choosingly, he was looking for paradise. Unchoosingly, he was mad with hatred of the world.

Well, the world is hateful. It is as hateful as Melville found it. He was not wrong in hating the world. *Delenda est Chicago*. He hated it to a pitch of madness, and not without reason.

But it's no good *persisting* in looking for paradise "regained".

Melville at his best invariably wrote from a sort of dream-self, so that events which he relates as actual fact have indeed a far deeper reference to his own soul, his own inner life.

So in *Typee* when he tells of his entry into the valley of the dread cannibals of Nukuheva. Down this narrow, steep, horrible dark gorge he slides and struggles as we struggle in a dream, or in the act of birth, to emerge in the green Eden of the Golden Age, the valley of the cannibal savages. This is a bit of birth-myth, or re-birth myth, on Melville's part—unconscious, no doubt, because his running under-consciousness was always mystical and symbolical. He wasn't aware that he was being mystical.

There he is then, in Typee, among the dreaded cannibal

savages. And they are gentle and generous with him, and he is truly in a sort of Eden.

Here at last is Rousseau's Child of Nature and Chateaubriand's Noble Savage called upon and found at home. Yes, Melville loves his savage hosts. He finds them gentle, laughing lambs compared to the ravening wolves of his white brothers, left behind in America and on an American whaleship.

The ugliest beast on earth is the white man, says Melville.

In short, Herman found in Typee the paradise he was looking for. It is true, the Marquesans were "immoral", but he rather liked that. Morality was too white a trick to take him in. Then again, they were cannibals. And it filled him with horror even to think of this. But the savages were very private and even fiercely reserved in their cannibalism, and he might have spared himself his shudder. No doubt he had partaken of the Christian Sacraments many a time. "This is my body, take and eat. This is my blood. Drink it in remembrance of me." And if the savages liked to partake of their sacrament without raising the transubstantiation quibble, and if they liked to say, directly: "This is thy body, which I take from thee and eat. This is thy blood, which I sip in annihilation of thee", why surely their sacred ceremony was as awe-inspiring as the one Jesus substituted. But Herman chose to be horrified. I confess, I am not horrified; though, of course, I am not on the spot. But the savage sacrament seems to me more valid than the Christian: less side-tracking about it. Thirdly, he was shocked by their wild methods of warfare. He died before the great European war, so his shock was comfortable.

Three little quibbles: morality, cannibal sacrament, and stone axes. You must have a fly even in Paradisal ointment. And the first was a ladybird.

But Paradise. He insists on it. Paradise. He could even go stark naked, as before the Apple episode. And his Fayaway, a laughing little Eve, naked with him, and hankering after no apple of knowledge, so long as he would just love her when he felt like it. Plenty to eat, needing no clothes to wear, sunny, happy people, sweet water to swim in: everything a man can want. Then why wasn't he happy along with the savages?

Because he wasn't.

He grizzled in secret, and wanted to escape.

He even pined for Home and Mother, the two things he had run away from as far as ships would carry him. HOME and MOTHER. The two things that were his damnation.

There on the island, where the golden-green great palm-trees chinked in the sun, and the elegant reed houses let the sea-breeze through, and people went naked and laughed a great deal, and Fayaway put flowers in his hair for him—great red hibiscus flowers, and frangipani—O God, why wasn't he happy? Why wasn't he?

Because he wasn't.

Well, it's hard to make a man happy.

But I should not have been happy either. One's soul seems under a vacuum, in the South Seas.

The truth of the matter is, one cannot go back. Some men can: renegade. But Melville couldn't go back: and Gauguin couldn't really go back: and I know now that I could never go back. Back towards the past, savage life. One cannot go back. It is one's destiny inside one.

There are these peoples, these "savages". One does not despise them. One does not feel superior. But there is a gulf. There is a gulf in time and being. I cannot commingle my being with theirs.

There they are, these South Sea Islanders, beautiful big men with their golden limbs and their laughing, graceful laziness. And they will call you brother, choose you as a brother. But why cannot one truly be brother?

There is an invisible hand grasps my heart and prevents it opening too much to these strangers. They are beautiful, they are like children, they are generous: but they are more than this. They are far off, and in their eyes is an easy darkness of the soft, uncreate past. In a way, they are uncreate. Far be it from me to assume any "white" superiority. But they are savages. They are gentle and laughing and physically very handsome. But it seems to me, that in living so far, through all our bitter centuries of civilization, we have still been living onwards, forwards. God knows it looks like a *cul de sac* now. But turn to the first negro, and then listen to your own soul. And your own soul will tell you that however false and foul our forms and systems are now, still, through the many centuries since Egypt, we have been living and struggling forwards along some road that is no road, and yet is a great life-development. We have struggled on, and on we must still go. We may have to smash things. Then let us smash. And our road may have to take a great swerve, that seems a retrogression.

But we can't go back. Whatever else the South Sea Islander is, he is centuries and centuries behind us in the life-struggle, the consciousness-struggle, the struggle of the soul into fulness. There is his woman, with her knotted hair and her dark, inchoate, slightly sardonic eyes. I like her, she is nice. But I would never want to touch her. I could not go back on myself so far. Back to their uncreate condition.

She has soft warm flesh, like warm mud. Nearer the reptile, the Saurian age. *Noli me tangere.*

We can't go back. We can't go back to the savages: not a stride. We can be in sympathy with them. We can take a great curve in their direction, onwards. But we cannot turn the current of our life backwards, back towards their soft warm twilight and uncreate mud. Not for a moment. If we do it for a moment, it makes us sick.

We can only do it when we are renegade. The renegade hates life itself. He wants the death of life. So these many "reformers" and "idealists" who glorify the savages in America. They are death-birds, life-haters. Renegades.

We can't go back, and Melville couldn't. Much as he hated the civilized humanity he knew. He couldn't go back to the savages; he wanted to, he tried to, and he couldn't.

Because, in the first place, it made him sick; it made him physically ill. He had something wrong with his leg, and this would not heal. It got worse and worse, during his four months on the island. When he escaped, he was in a deplorable condition—sick and miserable, ill, very ill.

Paradise!

But there you are. Try to go back to the savages, and you feel as if your very soul was decomposing inside you. That is what you feel in the South Seas, anyhow: as if your soul was decomposing inside you. And with any savages the same, if you try to go their way, take their current of sympathy.

Yet, as I say, we must make a great swerve in our

onward-going life-course now, to gather up again the savage
mysteries. But this does not mean going back on ourselves.

Going back to the savages made Melville sicker than anything. It made him feel as if he were decomposing. Worse
even than Home and Mother.

And that is what really happens. If you prostitute your
psyche by returning to the savages, you gradually go to
pieces. Before you can go back, you *have* to decompose.
And a white man decomposing is a ghastly sight. Even
Melville in Typee.

We have to go on, on, on, even if we must smash a way
ahead.

So Melville escaped, and threw a boat-hook full in the
throat of one of his dearest savage friends, and sank him,
because that savage was swimming in pursuit. That's how
he felt about the savages when they wanted to detain him.
He'd have murdered them one and all, vividly, rather than
be kept from escaping. Away from them—he must get
away from them—at any price.

And once he has escaped, immediately he begins to sigh
and pine for the "Paradise"—Home and Mother being at
the other end even of a whaling voyage.

When he really was Home with Mother, he found it
Purgatory. But Typee must have been even worse than
Purgatory, a soft hell, judging from the murderous frenzy
which possessed him to escape.

But once aboard the whaler that carried him off from
Nukuheva, he looked back and sighed for the Paradise he
had just escaped from in such a fever.

Poor Melville! He was determined Paradise existed. So
he was always in Purgatory.

He was born for Purgatory. Some souls are purgatorial
by destiny.

The very freedom of his Typee was a torture to him. Its
ease was slowly horrible to him. This time *he* was the fly in
the odorous tropical ointment.

He needed to fight. It was no good to him, the relaxation
of the non-moral tropics. He didn't really want Eden. He
wanted to fight. Like every American. To fight. But with
weapons of the spirit, not the flesh.

That was the top and bottom of it. His soul was in
revolt, writhing for ever in revolt. When he had something

definite to rebel against—like the bad conditions on a whaling ship—then he was much happier in his miseries. The mills of God were grinding inside him, and they needed something to grind on.

When they could grind on the injustice and folly of missionaries, or of brutal sea-captains, or of governments, he was easier. The mills of God were grinding inside him.

They are grinding inside every American. And they grind exceeding small.

Why? Heaven knows. But we've got to grind down our old forms, our old selves, grind them very very small, to nothingness. Whether a new somethingness will ever start, who knows? Meanwhile the mills of God grind on, in American Melville, and it was himself he ground small: himself and his wife, when he was married. For the present, the South Seas.

He escapes on to the craziest, most impossible of whaling ships. Lucky for us Melville makes it fantastic. It must have been pretty sordid.

And anyhow, on the crazy *Julia*, his leg, that would never heal in the paradise of Typee, began quickly to get well. His life was falling into its normal pulse. The drain back into past centuries was over.

Yet, oh, as he sails away from Nukuheva, on the voyage that will ultimately take him to America, oh, the acute and intolerable nostalgia he feels for the island he has left.

The past, the Golden Age of the past—what a nostalgia we all feel for it. Yet we don't want it when we get it. Try the South Seas.

Melville had to fight, fight against the existing world, against his own very self. Only he would never quite put the knife in the heart of his paradisal ideal. Somehow, somewhere, somewhen, love should be a fulfilment, and life should be a thing of bliss. That was his fixed ideal. Fata Morgana.

That was the pin he tortured himself on, like a pinned-down butterfly.

Love is never a fulfilment. Life is never a thing of continuous bliss. There is no paradise. Fight and laugh and feel bitter and feel bliss: and fight again. Fight, fight. That is life.

Why pin ourselves down on a paradisal ideal? It is only ourselves we torture.

Melville did have one great experience, getting away from humanity: the experience of the sea.

The South Sea Islands were not his great experience. They were a glamorous world outside New England. Outside. But it was the sea that was both outside and inside: the universal experience.

The book that follows on from *Typee* is *Omoo*.

Omoo is a fascinating book; picaresque, rascally, roving. Melville, as a bit of a beachcomber. The crazy ship *Julia* sails to Tahiti, and the mutinous crew are put ashore. Put in the Tahitian prison. It is good reading.

Perhaps Melville is at his best, his happiest, in *Omoo*. For once he is really reckless. For once he takes life as it comes. For once he is the gallant rascally epicurean, eating the world like a snipe, dirt and all baked into one *bonne bouche*.

For once he is really careless, roving with that scamp, Doctor Long Ghost. For once he is careless of his actions, careless of his morals, careless of his ideals: ironic, as the epicurean must be. The deep irony of your real scamp: your real epicurean of the moment.

But it was under the influence of the Long Doctor. This long and bony Scotsman was not a mere ne'er-do-well. He was a man of humorous desperation, throwing his life ironically away. Not a mere loose-kneed loafer, such as the South Seas seem to attract.

That is good about Melville: he never repents. Whatever he did, in Typee or in Doctor Long Ghost's wicked society, he never repented. If he ate his snipe, dirt and all, and enjoyed it at the time, he didn't have bilious bouts afterwards, which is good.

But it wasn't enough. The Long Doctor was really knocking about in a sort of despair. He let his ship drift rudderless.

Melville couldn't do this. For a time, yes. For a time, in this Long Doctor's company, he was rudderless and reckless. Good as an experience. But a man who will not abandon himself to despair or indifference cannot keep it up.

Melville would never abandon himself either to despair or indifference. He always cared. He always cared enough to hate missionaries, and to be touched by a real act of kindness. He always cared.

When he saw a white man really "gone savage", a white man with a blue shark tattooed over his brow, gone over to the savages, then Herman's whole being revolted. He couldn't bear it. He could not bear a renegade.

He enlisted at last on an American man-of-war. You have the record in *White Jacket*. He was back in civilization, but still at sea. He was in America, yet loose in the seas. Good regular days, after Doctor Long Ghost and the *Julia*.

As a matter of fact, a long thin chain was round Melville's ankle all the time, binding him to America, to civilization, to democracy, to the ideal world. It was a long chain, and it never broke. It pulled him back.

By the time he was twenty-five his wild oats were sown; his reckless wanderings were over. At the age of twenty-five he came back to Home and Mother, to fight it out at close quarters. For you can't fight it out by running away. When you have run a long way from Home and Mother, then you realize that the earth is round, and if you keep on running you'll be back on the same old doorstep,—like a fatality.

Melville came home to face out the long rest of his life. He married and had an ecstasy of a courtship and fifty years of disillusion.

He had just furnished his home with disillusions. No more Typees. No more paradises. No more Fayaways. A mother: a gorgon. A home: a torture box. A wife: a thing with clay feet. Life: a sort of disgrace. Fame: another disgrace, being patronized by common snobs who just know how to read.

The whole shameful business just making a man writhe.

Melville writhed for eighty years.

In his soul he was proud and savage.

But in his mind and will he wanted the perfect fulfilment of love; he wanted the lovey-doveyness of perfect mutual understanding.

A proud savage-souled man doesn't really want any perfect lovey-dovey fulfilment in love: no such nonsense. A mountain lion doesn't mate with a Persian cat; and when a grizzly bear roars after a mate, it is a she-grizzly he roars after—not after a silky sheep.

But Melville stuck to his ideal. He wrote *Pierre* to show that the more you try to be good the more you make a mess of things: that following righteousness is just disastrous. The better you are, the worse things turn out with you. The better you try to be, the bigger mess you make. Your very striving after righteousness only causes your own slow degeneration.

Well, it is true. No men are so evil to-day as the idealists, and no women half so evil as your earnest woman, who feels herself a power for good. It is inevitable. After a certain point, the ideal goes dead and rotten. The old pure ideal becomes in itself an impure thing of evil. Charity becomes pernicious, the spirit itself becomes foul. The meek are evil. The pure in heart have base, subtle revulsions: like Dostoevsky's Idiot. The whole Sermon on the Mount becomes a litany of white vice.

What then?

It's our own fault. It was *we* who set up the ideals. And if we are such fools, that we aren't able to kick over our ideals in time, the worse for us.

Look at Melville's eighty long years of writhing. And to the end he writhed on the ideal pin.

From the "perfect woman lover" he passed on to the "perfect friend". He looked and looked for the perfect man friend.

Couldn't find him.

Marriage was a ghastly disillusion to him, because he looked for perfect marriage.

Friendship never even made a real start in him—save perhaps his half-sentimental love for Jack Chase, in *White Jacket*.

Yet to the end he pined for this: a perfect relationship; perfect mating; perfect mutual understanding. A perfect friend.

Right to the end he could never accept the fact that *perfect* relationships cannot be. Each soul is alone, and the aloneness of each soul is a double barrier to perfect relationship between two beings.

Each soul *should* be alone. And in the end the desire for a "perfect relationship" is just a vicious, unmanly craving. *"Tous nos malheurs viennent de ne pouvoir être seuls."*

Melville, however, refused to draw his conclusion. *Life*

was wrong, he said. He refused Life. But he stuck to his ideal of perfect relationship, possible perfect love. The world *ought* to be a harmonious loving place. And it *can't* be. So life itself is wrong.

It is silly arguing. Because, after all, only temporary man sets up the "oughts".

The world ought *not* to be a harmonious loving place. It ought to be a place of fierce discord and intermittent harmonies: which it is.

Love ought *not* to be perfect. It ought to have perfect moments, and wildernesses of thorn bushes—which it has.

A "perfect" relationship ought *not* to be possible. Every relationship should have its absolute limits, its absolute reserves, essential to the singleness of the soul in each person. A truly perfect relationship is one in which each party leaves great tracts unknown in the other party.

No two persons can meet at more than a few points, consciously. If two people can just be together fairly often, so that the presence of each is a sort of balance to the other, that is the basis of perfect relationship. There must be true separatenesses as well.

Melville was, at the core, a mystic and an idealist.

Perhaps, so am I.

And he stuck to his ideal guns.

I abandon mine.

He was a mystic who raved because the old ideal guns shot havoc. The guns of the "noble spirit". Of "ideal love"

I say, let the old guns rot.

Get new ones, and shoot straight.

CHAPTER XI

HERMAN MELVILLE'S "MOBY DICK"

MOBY DICK, *or the White Whale.*
A hunt. The last great hunt.
For what?
For Moby Dick, the huge white sperm whale: who is
old, hoary, monstrous, and swims alone; who is unspeak-
ably terrible in his wrath, having so often been attacked;
and snow-white.
Of course he is a symbol.
Of what?
I doubt if even Melville knew exactly. That's the best
of it.
He is warm-blooded, he is loveable. He is lonely Leviathan, not a Hobbes sort. Or is he?
But he is warm-blooded and loveable. The South Sea
Islanders, and Polynesians, and Malays, who worship shark,
or crocodile, or weave endless frigate-bird distortions, why
did they never worship the whale? So big!
Because the whale is not wicked. He doesn't bite. And
their gods had to bite.
He's not a dragon. He is Leviathan. He never coils like
the Chinese dragon of the sun. He's not a serpent of the
waters. He is warm-blooded, a mammal. And hunted,
hunted down.
It is a great book.
At first you are put off by the style. It reads like journal-
ism. It seems spurious. You feel Melville is trying to put
something over you. It won't do.
And Melville really is a bit sententious: aware of himself, self-conscious, putting something over even himself.
But then it's not easy to get into the swing of a piece of
deep mysticism when you just set out with a story.
Nobody can be more clownish, more clumsy and senten-
tiously in bad taste, than Herman Melville, even in a great

145

book like *Moby Dick*. He preaches and holds forth because he's not sure of himself. And he holds forth, often, so amateurishly.

The artist was so *much* greater than the man. The man is rather a tiresome New Englander of the ethical mystical-transcendentalist sort: Emerson, Longfellow, Hawthorne, etc. So unrelieved, the solemn ass even in humour. So hopelessly *au grand sérieux*, you feel like saying: Good God, what does it matter? If life is a tragedy, or a farce, or a disaster, or anything else, what do I care! Let life be what it likes. Give me a drink, that's what I want just now.

For my part, life is so many things I don't care what it is. It's not my affair to sum it up. Just now it's a cup of tea. This morning it was wormwood and gall. Hand me the sugar.

One wearies of the *grand sérieux*. There's something false about it. And that's Melville. Oh dear, when the solemn ass brays! brays! brays!

But he was a deep, great artist, even if he was rather a sententious man. He was a real American in that he always felt his audience in front of him. But when he ceases to be American, when he forgets all audience, and gives us his sheer apprehension of the world, then he is wonderful, his book commands a stillness in the soul, an awe.

In his "human" self, Melville is almost dead. That is, he hardly reacts to human contacts any more; or only ideally: or just for a moment. His human-emotional self is almost played out. He is abstract, self-analytical and abstracted. And he is more spell-bound by the strange slidings and collidings of Matter than by the things men do. In this he is like Dana. It is the material elements he really has to do with. His drama is with them. He was a futurist long before futurism found paint. The sheer naked slidings of the elements. And the human soul experiencing it all. So often, it is almost over the border: psychiatry. Almost spurious. Yet so great.

It is the same old thing as in all Americans. They keep their old-fashioned ideal frock-coat on, and an old-fashioned silk hat, while they do the most impossible things. There you are: you see Melville hugged in bed by a huge tattooed South Sea Islander, and solemnly offering burnt offering to this savage's little idol, and his ideal frock-coat just hides his shirt-tails and prevents us from seeing his bare posterior as he salaams, while his ethical silk hat sits correctly over his brow the while. That is so typically American: doing the most impossible things without taking off their spiritual get-up. Their ideals are like armour which has rusted in, and will never more come off. And meanwhile in Melville his bodily knowledge moves naked, a living quick among the stark elements. For with sheer physical vibrational sensitiveness, like a marvellous wireless-station, he registers the effects of the outer world. And he records also, almost beyond pain or pleasure, the extreme transitions of the isolated, far-driven soul, the soul which is now alone, without any real human contact.

The first days in New Bedford introduce the only human being who really enters into the book, namely, Ishmael, the "I" of the book. And then the moment's heart's-brother, Queequeg, the tattooed, powerful South Sea harpooner, whom Melville loves as Dana loves "Hope". The advent of Ishmael's bedmate is amusing and unforgettable. But later the two swear "marriage", in the language of the savages. For Queequeg has opened again the flood-gates of love and human connexion in Ishmael.

"As I sat there in that now lonely room, the fire burning low, in that mild stage when, after its first intensity has warmed the air, it then only glows to be looked at; the evening shades and phantoms gathering round the casements, and peering in upon us silent, solitary twain: I began to be sensible of strange feelings. I felt a melting in me. No more my splintered heart and maddened hand were turned against the wolfish world. This soothing savage had redeemed it. There he sat, his very indifference speaking a nature in which there lurked no civilized hypocrisies and bland deceits. Wild he was; a very sight of sights to see; yet I began to feel myself mysteriously drawn towards him."—So they smoked together, and are clasped in each other's arms. The friendship is finally sealed when Ishmael offers sacrifice to Queequeg's little idol, Gogo.

"I was a good Christian, born and bred in the bosom of the infallible Presbyterian Church. How then could I unite with the idolater in worshipping his piece of wood? But what is worship?—to do the will of God—*that* is worship. And what is the will of God?—to do to my fellow man what I would have my fellow man do to me—*that* is the will of God."—Which sounds like Benjamin Franklin, and is hopelessly bad theology. But it is real American logic. "Now Queequeg is my fellow man. And what do I wish that this Queequeg would do to me? Why, unite with me in my particular Presbyterian form of worship. Consequently, I must unite with him; ergo, I must turn idolater. So I kindled the shavings; helped prop up the innocent little idol; offered him burnt biscuit with Queequeg; salaamed before him twice or thrice; kissed his nose; and that done, we undressed and went to bed, at peace with our own consciences and all the world. But we did not go to sleep without some little chat. How it is I know not; but there is no place like bed for confidential disclosures between friends. Man and wife, they say, open the very bottom of their souls to each other; and some old couples often lie and chat over old times till nearly morning. Thus, then, lay I and Queequeg—a cosy, loving pair——"

You would think this relation with Queequeg meant something to Ishmael. But no. Queequeg is forgotten like yesterday's newspaper. Human things are only momentary excitements or amusements to the American Ishmael. Ishmael, the hunted. But much more Ishmael the hunter. What's a Queequeg? What's a wife? The white whale must be hunted down. Queequeg must be just "KNOWN", then dropped into oblivion.

And what in the name of fortune is the white whale?

Elsewhere Ishmael says he loved Queequeg's eyes: "large, deep eyes, fiery black and bold." No doubt like Poe, he wanted to get the "clue" to them. That was all.

The two men go over from New Bedford to Nantucket, and there sign on to the Quaker whaling ship, the *Pequod*. It is all strangely fantastic, phantasmagoric. The voyage of the soul. Yet curiously a real whaling voyage, too. We pass on into the midst of the sea with this strange ship and its incredible crew. The Argonauts were mild lambs in comparison. And Ulysses went *defeating* the Circes and overcoming the wicked hussies of the isles. But the *Pequod's* crew is a collection of maniacs fanatically hunting down a lonely, harmless white whale.

As a soul history, it makes one angry. As a sea yarn, it is marvellous: there is always something a bit over the mark, in sea yarns. Should be. Then again the masking up of actual seaman's experience with sonorous mysticism sometimes gets on one's nerves. And again, as a revelation of destiny the book is too deep even for sorrow. Profound beyond feeling.

You are some time before you are allowed to see the captain, Ahab: the mysterious Quaker. Oh, it is a God-fearing Quaker ship.

Ahab, the captain. The captain of the soul.

> "I am the master of my fate,
> I am the captain of my soul!"

Ahab!

"Oh, captain, my captain, our fearful trip is done."

The gaunt Ahab, Quaker, mysterious person, only shows himself after some days at sea. There's a secret about him! What?

Oh, he's a portentous person. He stumps about on an ivory stump, made from sea-ivory. Moby Dick, the great white whale, tore off Ahab's leg at the knee, when Ahab was attacking him.

Quite right, too. Should have torn off both his legs, and a bit more besides.

But Ahab doesn't think so. Ahab is now a monomaniac. Moby Dick is his monomania. Moby Dick must DIE, or Ahab can't live any longer. Ahab is atheist by this.

All right.

This *Pequod*, ship of the American soul, has three mates.

1. Starbuck: Quaker, Nantucketer, a good responsible man of reason, forethought, intrepidity, what is called a dependable man. At the bottom, *afraid*.

2. Stubb: "Fearless as fire, and as mechanical." Insists on being reckless and jolly on every occasion. Must be afraid too, really.

3. Flask: Stubborn, obstinate, without imagination. To him "the wondrous whale was but a species of magnified mouse or water-rat——"

There you have them: a maniac captain and his three mates, three splendid seamen, admirable whalemen, first-class men at their job.

America!

It is rather like Mr. Wilson and his admirable, "efficient"

150 STUDIES IN CLASSIC AMERICAN LITERATURE

crew, at the Peace Conference. Except that none of the Pequodders took their wives along.

A maniac captain of the soul, and three eminently practical mates.

America!

Then such a crew. Renegades, castaways, cannibals: Ishmael, Quakers.

America!

Three giant harpooners, to spear the great white whale.

1. Queequeg, the South Sea Islander, all tattooed, big and powerful.

2. Tashtego, the Red Indian of the sea-coast, where the Indian meets the sea.

3. Daggoo, the huge black negro.

There you have them, three savage races, under the American flag, the maniac captain, with their great keen harpoons, ready to spear the white whale.

And only after many days at sea does Ahab's own boat-crew appear on deck. Strange, silent, secret, black-garbed Malays, fire-worshipping Parsees. These are to man Ahab's boat, when it leaps in pursuit of that whale.

What do you think of the ship *Pequod*, the ship of the soul of an American?

Many races, many peoples, many nations, under the Stars and Stripes. Beaten with many stripes.

Seeing stars sometimes.

And in a mad ship, under a mad captain, in a mad, fanatic's hunt.

For what?

For Moby Dick, the great white whale.

But splendidly handled. Three splendid mates. The whole thing practical, eminently practical in its working. American industry!

And all this practicality in the service of a mad, mad chase.

Melville manages to keep it a real whaling ship, on a real cruise, in spite of all fantastics. A wonderful, wonderful voyage. And a beauty that is so surpassing only because of the author's awful flounderings in mystical waters. He wanted to get metaphysically deep. And he got deeper than metaphysics. It is a surpassingly beautiful book, with an awful meaning, and bad jolts.

It is interesting to compare Melville with Dana, about the albatross—Melville a bit sententious. "I remember the first albatross I ever saw. It was during a prolonged gale in waters hard upon the Antarctic seas. From my forenoon watch below I ascended to the overcrowded deck, and there, lashed upon the main hatches, I saw a regal feathered thing of unspotted whiteness, and with a hooked Roman bill sublime. At intervals it arched forth its vast, archangel wings—wondrous throbbings and flutterings shook it. Though bodily unharmed, it uttered cries, as some King's ghost in supernatural distress. Through its inexpressible strange eyes methought I peeped to secrets not below the heavens—the white thing was so white, its wings so wide, and in those for ever exiled waters, I had lost the miserable warping memories of traditions and of towns. I assert then, that in the wondrous bodily whiteness of the bird chiefly lurks the secret of the spell——"

Melville's albatross is a prisoner, caught by a bait on a hook.

Well, I have seen an albatross, too: following us in waters hard upon the Antarctic, too, south of Australia. And in the Southern winter. And the ship, a P. and O. boat, nearly empty. And the lascar crew shivering.

The bird with its long, long wings following, then leaving us. No one knows till they have tried, how lost, how lonely those Southern waters are. And glimpses of the Australian coast.

It makes one feel that our day is only a day. That in the dark of the night ahead other days stir fecund, when we have lapsed from existence.

Who knows how utterly we shall lapse.

But Melville keeps up his disquisition about "whiteness". The great abstract fascinated him. The abstract where we end, and cease to be. White or black. Our white, abstract end!

Then again it is lovely to be at sea on the *Pequod*, with never a grain of earth to us.

"It was a cloudy, sultry afternoon; the seamen were lazily lounging about the decks, or vacantly gazing over into the lead-coloured waters. Queequeg and I were mildly employed weaving what is called a sword-mat, for an additional lashing to our boat. So still and subdued, and yet

somehow preluding was all the scene, and such an incanta-
tion of reverie lurked in the air that each silent sailor
seemed resolved into his own invisible self——"

In the midst of this preluding silence came the first cry:
"There she blows! there! there! there! She blows!" And
then comes the first chase, a marvellous piece of true sea-
writing, the sea, and sheer sea-beings on the chase, sea-
creatures chased. There is scarcely a taint of earth—pure
sea-motion.

" 'Give way, men,' whispered Starbuck, drawing still
further aft the sheet of his sail; 'there is time to kill a fish yet
before the squall comes. There's white water again!—Close
to!—Spring!' Soon after, two cries in quick succession on
each side of us denoted that the other boats had got fast;
but hardly were they overheard, when with a lightning-
like hurtling whisper Starbuck said: 'Stand up!' and
Queequeg, harpoon in hand, sprang to his feet.—Though
not one of the oarsmen was then facing the life and death
peril so close to them ahead, yet, their eyes on the intense
countenance of the mate in the stern of the boat, they
knew that the imminent instant had come; they heard, too,
an enormous wallowing sound, as of fifty elephants stirring
in their litter. Meanwhile the boat was still booming
through the mist, the waves curbing and hissing around us
like the erected crests of enraged serpents.

" 'That's his hump. *There! There*, give it to him!' whispered Starbuck.—A short rushing sound leapt out of the
boat; it was the darted iron of Queequeg. Then all in one
welded motion came a push from astern, while forward
the boat seemed striking on a ledge; the sail collapsed and
exploded; a gush of scalding vapour shot up near by; something rolled and tumbled like an earthquake beneath us.
The whole crew were half-suffocated as they were tossed
helter-skelter into the white curling cream of the squall.
Squall, whale, and harpoon had all blended together; and
the whale, merely grazed by the iron, escaped——"

Melville is a master of violent, chaotic physical motion;
he can keep up a whole wild chase without a flaw. He is as
perfect at creating stillness. The ship is cruising on the
Carrol Ground, south of St. Helena.—"It was while gliding
through these latter waters that one serene and moonlight
night, when all the waves rolled by like scrolls of silver;

and by their soft, suffusing seethings, made what seemed a silvery silence, not a solitude; on such a silent night a silvery jet was seen far in advance of the white bubbles at the bow——"

Then there is the description of brit. "Steering north-eastward from the Crozetts we fell in with vast meadows of brit, the minute, yellow substance upon which the Right Whale largely feeds. For leagues and leagues it undulated round us, so that we seemed to be sailing through bound-less fields of ripe and golden wheat. On the second day, numbers of Right Whales were seen, who, secure from the attack of a Sperm Whaler like the *Pequod*, with open jaws sluggishly swam through the brit, which, adhering to the fringing fibres of that wondrous Venetian blind in their mouths, was in that manner separated from the water that escaped at the lip. As moving mowers who, side by side, slowly and seethingly advance their scythes through the long wet grass of the marshy meads; even so these monsters swam, making a strange, grassy, cutting sound; and leaving behind them endless swaths of blue on the yellow sea. But it was only the sound they made as they parted the brit which at all reminded one of mowers. Seen from the mast-heads, especially when they paused and were stationary for a while, their vast black forms looked more like lifeless masses of rock than anything else——"

This beautiful passage brings us to the apparition of the squid.

"Slowly wading through the meadows of brit, the *Pequod* still held her way northeastward towards the island of Java; a gentle air impelling her keel, so that in the sur-rounding serenity her three tall, tapering masts mildly waved to that languid breeze, as three mild palms on a plain. And still, at wide intervals, in the silvery night, that lonely, alluring jet would be seen.

"But one transparent-blue morning, when a stillness almost preternatural spread over the sea, however unattended with any stagnant calm; when the long burnished sunglade on the waters seemed a golden finger laid across them, enjoin-ing secrecy; when all the slippered waves whispered together as they softly ran on; in this profound hush of the visible sphere a strange spectre was seen by Daggoo from the main-mast head.

"In the distance, a great white mass lazily rose, and rising higher and higher, and disentangling itself from the azure, at last gleamed before our prow like a snow-slide, new slid from the hills. Thus glistening for a moment, as slowly it subsided, and sank. Then once more arose, and silently gleamed. It seemed not a whale; and yet, is this Moby Dick? thought Daggoo——"

The boats were lowered and pulled to the scene.

"In the same spot where it sank, once more it slowly rose. Almost forgetting for the moment all thoughts of Moby Dick, we now gazed at the most wondrous phenomenon which the secret seas have hitherto revealed to mankind. A vast pulpy mass, furlongs in length and breadth, of a glancing cream-colour, lay floating on the water, innumerable long arms radiating from its centre, and curling and twisting like a nest of anacondas, as if blindly to clutch at any hapless object within reach. No perceptible face or front did it have; no conceivable token of either sensation or instinct; but undulated there on the billows, an unearthly, formless, chance-like apparition of life. And with a low sucking it slowly disappeared again."

The following chapters, with their account of whale hunts, the killing, the stripping, the cutting up, are magnificent records of actual happening. Then comes the queer tale of the meeting of the *Jeroboam*, a whaler met at sea, all of whose men were under the domination of a religious maniac, one of the ship's hands. There are detailed descriptions of the actual taking of the sperm oil from a whale's head. Dilating on the smallness of the brain of a sperm whale, Melville significantly remarks—"for I believe that much of a man's character will be found betokened in his backbone. I would rather feel your spine than your skull, whoever you are——" And of the whale, he adds:

"For, viewed in this light, the wonderful comparative smallness of his brain proper is more than compensated by the wonderful comparative magnitude of his spinal cord."

In among the rush of terrible, awful hunts, come touches of pure beauty.

"As the three boats lay there on that gently rolling sea, gazing down into its eternal blue noon; and as not a single groan or cry of any sort, nay not so much as a ripple or a thought, came up from its depths; what landsman would have thought that beneath all that silence and placidity the utmost monster of the seas was writhing and wrenching in agony!"

Perhaps the most stupendous chapter is the one called *The Grand Armada*, at the beginning of Volume III. The *Pequod* was drawing through the Sunda Straits towards Java when she came upon a vast host of sperm whales. "Broad on both bows, at a distance of two or three miles, and forming a great semicircle embracing one-half of the level horizon, a continuous chain of whale-jets were upplaying and sparkling in the noonday air." Chasing this great herd, past the Straits of Sunda, themselves chased by Javan pirates, the whalers race on. Then the boats are lowered. At last that curious state of inert irresolution came over the whales, when they were, as the seamen say, gallied. Instead of forging ahead in huge martial array they swam violently hither and thither, a surging sea of whales, no longer moving on. Starbuck's boat, made fast to a whale, is towed in amongst this howling Leviathan chaos. In mad career it cockles through the boiling surge of monsters, till it is brought into a clear lagoon in the very centre of the vast, mad, terrified herd. There a sleek, pure calm reigns. There the females swam in peace, and the young whales came snuffing tamely at the boat, like dogs. And there the astonished seamen watched the love-making of these amazing monsters, mammals, now in rut far down in the sea— "But far beneath this wondrous world upon the surface, another and still stranger world met our eyes, as we gazed over the side. For, suspended in these watery vaults, floated the forms of the nursing mothers of the whales, and those that by their enormous girth seemed shortly to become mothers. The lake, as I have hinted, was to a considerable depth exceedingly transparent; and as human infants while sucking will calmly and fixedly gaze away from the breast, as if leading two different lives at a time; and while yet drawing moral nourishment, be still spiritually feasting upon some unearthly reminiscence, even so did the young of these whales seem looking up towards us, but not at us, as if we were but a bit of gulf-weed in their newborn sight. Floating on their sides, the mothers also seemed quietly eyeing us.—Some of the subtlest secrets of the seas seemed divulged to us in this enchanted pond. We saw young Leviathan amours in the deep. And thus, though surrounded by circle upon circle of consternation and affrights, did these inscrutable creatures at the centre freely and fearlessly indulge in all peaceful concernments; yea, serenely revelled in dalliance and delight——"

There is something really overwhelming in these whalehunts, almost superhuman or inhuman, bigger than life, more terrific than human activity. The same with the chapter on ambergris: it is so curious, so real, yet so unearthly. And again in the chapter called *The Cassock* —surely the oldest piece of phallicism in all the world's literature.

After this comes the amazing account of the Try-works, when the ship is turned into the sooty, oily factory in midocean, and the oil is extracted from the blubber. In the night of the red furnace burning on deck, at sea, Melville has his startling experience of reversion. He is at the helm, but has turned to watch the fire: when suddenly he feels the ship rushing backward from him, in mystic reversion— "Uppermost was the impression, that whatever swift, rushing thing I stood on was not so much bound to any haven ahead, as rushing from all havens astern. A stark bewildering feeling, as of death, came over me. Convulsively my hands grasped the tiller, but with the crazy conceit that the tiller was, somehow, in some enchanted way, inverted. My God! What is the matter with me, I thought!"

This dream-experience is a real soul-experience. He ends with an injunction to all men, not to gaze on the red fire when its redness makes all things look ghastly. It seems to him that his gazing on fire has evoked this horror of reversion, undoing.

Perhaps it had. He was water-born.

After some unhealthy work on the ship, Queequeg caught a fever and was like to die. "How he wasted and wasted in those few, long-lingering days, till there seemed but little left of him but his frame and tattooing. But as all else in him thinned, and his cheek-bones grew sharper, his eyes, nevertheless, seemed growing fuller and fuller; they took on a strangeness of lustre; and mildly but deeply looked out at you there from his sickness, a wondrous testimony to that immortal health in him which could not die, or be weakened. And like circles on the water, which as they grow fainter, expand; so his eyes seemed rounding and rounding, like the circles of Eternity. An awe that cannot be named would steal over you as you sat by the side of this waning savage——"

But Queequeg did not die—and the *Pequod* emerges from the Eastern Straits, into the full Pacific. "To any meditative Magian rover, this serene Pacific once beheld, must ever after be the sea of his adoption. It rolls the midmost waters of the world——"

In this Pacific the fights go on: "It was far down the afternoon, and when all the spearings of the crimson fight were done, and floating in the lovely sunset sea and sky, sun and whale both stilly died together; then such a sweetness and such a plaintiveness, such inwreathing orisons curled up in that rosy air, that it almost seemed as if far over from the deep green convent valleys of the Manila isles, the Spanish land-breeze had gone to sea, freighted with these vesper hymns. Soothed again, but only soothed to deeper gloom, Ahab, who had sterned off from the whale, sat intently watching his final wanings from the now tranquil boat. For that strange spectacle, observable in all sperm whales dying—the turning of the head sunwards, and so expiring—that strange spectacle, beheld of such a placid evening, somehow to Ahab conveyed wondrousness unknown before. 'He turns and turns him to it; how slowly, but how steadfastly, his homage-rendering and invoking brow, with his last dying motions. He too worships fire . . . '"

So Ahab soliloquizes: and so the warm-blooded whale turns for the last time to the sun, which begot him in the waters.

But as we see in the next chapter, it is the Thunder-fire which Ahab really worships: that living sundering fire of which he bears the brand, from head to foot; it is storm, the electric storm of the *Pequod*, when the corposants burn in high, tapering flames of supernatural pallor upon the masthead, and when the compass is reversed. After this all is fatality. Life itself seems mystically reversed. In these hunters of Moby Dick there is nothing but madness and possession. The captain, Ahab, moves hand in hand with the poor imbecile negro boy, pip, who has been so cruelly demented, left swimming alone in the vast sea. It is the imbecile child of the sun hand in hand with the northern monomaniac, captain and master.

The voyage surges on. They meet one ship, then another. It is all ordinary day-routine, and yet all is a tension of pure madness and horror, the approaching horror of the last fight. "Hither and thither, on high, glided the snow-white wings of small unspecked birds; these were the gentle thoughts of the feminine air; but to and fro in the deeps, far down in the bottomless blue, rushed mighty leviathans, sword-fish and sharks; and these were the strong, troubled, murderous thinkings of the masculine sea——" On this day Ahab confesses his weariness, the weariness of his burden. "But do I look very old, so very, very old, Starbuck? I feel deadly faint, and bowed, and humped, as though I were Adam staggering beneath the piled centuries since Paradise——" It is the Gethsemane of Ahab, before the last fight: the Gethsemane of the human soul seeking the last self-conquest, the last attainment of extended consciousness—infinite consciousness.

At last they sight the whale. Ahab sees him from his hoisted perch at the masthead—"From this height the whale was now seen some mile or so ahead, at every roll of the sea revealing his high, sparkling hump, and regularly jetting his silent spout into the air."

The boats are lowered, to draw near the white whale. "At length the breathless hunter came so nigh his seemingly unsuspectful prey that his entire dazzling hump was distinctly visible, sliding along the sea as if an isolated thing, and continually set in a revolving ring of finest, fleecy, greenish foam. He saw the vast involved wrinkles of the slightly projecting head, beyond. Before it, far out on the soft, Turkish rugged waters, went the glistening white shadow from his broad, milky forehead, a musical rippling playfully accompanying the shade; and behind, the blue waters interchangeably flowed over the moving valley of his steady wake; and on either side bright bubbles arose and danced by his side. But these were broken again by the light toes of hundreds of gay fowl softly feathering the sea, alternate with their fitful flight; and like to some flagstaff rising from the pointed hull of an argosy, the tall but shattered pole of a recent lance projected from the white whale's back; and at intervals one of the clouds of soft-toed fowls hovering, and to and fro shimmering like a canopy over the fish, silently perched and rocked on this pole, the long tail-feathers streaming like pennons.

"A gentle joyousness—a mighty mildness of repose in swiftness, invested the gliding whale——"

The fight with the whale is too wonderful, and too awful, to be quoted apart from the book. It lasted three days. The fearful sight, on the third day, of the torn body of the Parsee harpooner, lost on the previous day, now seen lashed on to the flanks of the white whale by the tangle of har-poon lines, has a mystic dream-horror. The awful and infuri-ated whale turns upon the ship, symbol of this civilized world of ours. He smites her with a fearful shock. And a few minutes later, from the last of the fighting whale-boats comes the cry : " 'The ship! Great God, where is the ship?' Soon they, through dim, bewildering mediums, saw her sidelong fading phantom, as in the gaseous Fata Morgana; only the uppermost masts out of the water; while fixed by infatuation, or fidelity, or fate, to their once lofty perches, the pagan harpooners still maintained their sinking look-outs on the sea. And now concentric circles seized the lone boat itself, and all its crew, and each floating oar, and every lance-pole, and spinning, animate and inanimate, all round and round in one vortex, carried the smallest chip of the *Pequod* out of sight——"

The bird of heaven, the eagle, St. John's bird, the Red Indian bird, the American, goes down with the ship, nailed by Tashtego's hammer, the hammer of the American Indian. The eagle of the spirit. Sunk!

"Now small fowls flew screaming over the yet yawning gulf; a sullen white surf beat against its steep sides; then all collapsed; and the great shroud of the sea rolled on as it rolled five thousand years ago."

So ends one of the strangest and most wonderful books in the world, closing up its mystery and its tortured sym-bolism. It is an epic of the sea such as no man has equalled; and it is a book of esoteric symbolism of profound signifi-cance, and of considerable tiresomeness.

But it is a great book, a very great book, the greatest book of the sea ever written. It moves awe in the soul.

The terrible fatality.

Fatality.

Doom.

Doom! Doom! Doom! Something seems to whisper it in the very dark trees of America. Doom!

Doom of what?

Doom of our white day. We are doomed, doomed. And the doom is in America. The doom of our white day.

Ah, well, if my day is doomed, and I am doomed with my day, it is something greater than I which dooms me, so I accept my doom as a sign of the greatness which is more than I am.

Melville knew. He knew his race was doomed. His white soul, doomed. His great white epoch, doomed. Himself, doomed. The idealist, doomed. The spirit, doomed.

The reversion. "Not so much bound to any haven ahead, as rushing from all havens astern."

That great horror of ours! It is our civilization rushing from all havens astern.

The last ghastly hunt. The White Whale.

What then is Moby Dick? He is the deepest blood-being of the white race; he is our deepest blood-nature.

And he is hunted, hunted, hunted by the maniacal fanaticism of our white mental consciousness. We want to hunt him down. To subject him to our will. And in this maniacal conscious hunt of ourselves we get dark races and pale to help us, red, yellow, and black, east and west, Quaker and fire-worshipper, we get them all to help us in this ghastly maniacal hunt which is our doom and our suicide.

The last phallic being of the white man. Hunted into the death of upper consciousness and the ideal will. Our blood-self subjected to our will. Our blood-consciousness sapped by a parasitic mental or ideal consciousness.

Hot-blooded sea-born Moby Dick. Hunted by mono-maniacs of the idea.

Oh God, oh God, what next, when the *Pequod* has sunk?

She sank in the war, and we are all flotsam.

Now what next?

Who knows? *Quien sabe? Quien sabe, señor?*

Neither Spanish nor Saxon America has any answer.

The *Pequod* went down. And the *Pequod* was the ship of the white American soul. She sank, taking with her negro and Indian and Polynesian, Asiatic and Quaker and good, businesslike Yankees and Ishmael: she sank all the lot of them.

Boom! as Vachel Lindsay would say.

To use the words of Jesus, IT IS FINISHED.

Consummatum est!

But *Moby Dick* was first published in 1851. If the Great White Whale sank the ship of the Great White Soul in 1851, what's been happening ever since?

Post-mortem effects, presumably.

Because, in the first centuries, Jesus was Cetus, the Whale. And the Christians were the little fishes. Jesus, the Redeemer, was Cetus, Leviathan. And all the Christians all his little fishes.

CHAPTER XII

WHITMAN

Post-mortem effects?

But what of Walt Whitman?

The "good grey poet".

Was he a ghost, with all his physicality?

The good grey poet.

Post-mortem effects. Ghosts.

A certain ghoulish insistency. A certain horrible pottage of human parts. A certain stridency and portentousness. A luridness about his beatitudes.

Democracy! These States! Eidolons! Lovers, Endless Lovers!

One Identity!

One Identity!

I am he that aches with Amorous Love.

Do you believe me, when I say post-mortem effects?

When the *Pequod* went down, she left many a rank and dirty steamboat still fussing in the seas. The *Pequod* sinks with all her souls, but their bodies rise again to man innumerable tramp steamers, and ocean-crossing liners. Corpses.

What we mean is that people may go on, keep on, and rush on, without souls. They have their ego and their will; that is enough to keep them going.

So that you see, the sinking of the *Pequod* was only a metaphysical tragedy after all. The world goes on just the same. The ship of the *soul* is sunk. But the machine-manipulating body works just the same: digests, chews gum, admires Botticelli and aches with amorous love.

I am he that aches with Amorous Love.

What do you make of that? I am he that aches. First generalization. First uncomfortable universalization. With amorous love! Oh, God! Better a bellyache. A bellyache is at least specific. But the ache of Amorous Love!

Think of having that under your skin. All that!

I AM HE THAT ACHES WITH AMOROUS LOVE.

Walter, leave off. You are not HE. You are just a limited Walter. And your ache doesn't include all Amorous Love, by any means. If you ache you only ache with a small bit of amorous love, and there's so much more stays outside the cover of your ache, that you might be a bit milder about it.

I AM HE THAT ACHES WITH AMOROUS LOVE.

CHUFF! CHUFF! CHUFF!

CHU-CHU-CHU-CHU-CHUFF!

Reminds one of a steam-engine. A locomotive. They're the only things that seem to me to ache with amorous love. All that steam inside them. Forty million foot-pounds pressure. The ache of AMOROUS LOVE. Steam-pressure. CHUFF!

An ordinary man aches with love for Belinda, or his Native Land, or the Ocean, or the Stars, or the Oversoul: if he feels that an ache is in the fashion.

It takes a steam-engine to ache with AMOROUS LOVE. All of it.

Walt was really too superhuman. The danger of the superman is that he is mechanical.

They talk of his "splendid animality". Well, he'd got it on the brain, if that's the place for animality.

"I am he that aches with amorous love:
  Does the earth gravitate, does not all matter, aching, attract all matter?
  So the body of me to all I meet or know."

What can be more mechanical? The difference between life and matter is that life, living things, living creatures, have the instinct of turning right away from *some* matter, and of blissfully ignoring the bulk of most matter, and of turning towards only some certain bits of specially selected matter. As for living creatures all helplessly hurtling together into one great snowball, why, most very living creatures spend the greater part of their time getting out of the sight, smell or sound of the rest of living creatures. Even bees only cluster on their own queen. And that is sickening enough. Fancy all white humanity clustering on one another like a lump of bees.

No, Walt, you give yourself away. Matter *does* gravitate,

helplessly. But men are tricky-tricksy, and they shy all sorts of ways.

Matter gravitates because it *is* helpless and mechanical.

And if you gravitate the same, if the body of you gravitates to all you meet or know, why, something must have gone seriously wrong with you. You must have broken your mainspring.

You must have fallen also into mechanization.

Your Moby Dick must be really dead. That lonely phallic monster of the individual you. Dead mentalized.

I only know that my body doesn't by any means gravitate to all I meet or know. I find I can shake hands with a few people. But most I wouldn't touch with a long prop.

Your mainspring is broken, Walt Whitman. The mainspring of your own individuality. And so you run down with a great whirr, merging with everything.

You have killed your isolate Moby Dick. You have mentalized your deep sensual body, and that's the death of it.

I am everything and everything is me and so we're all One in One Identity, like the Mundane Egg, which has been addled quite a while.

"Whoever you are, to endless announcements——"
"And of these one and all I weave the song of myself."

Do you? Well then, it just shows you haven't *got* any self. It's a mush, not a woven thing. A hotch-potch, not a tissue. Your self.

Oh, Walter, Walter, what have you done with it? What have you done with yourself? With your own individual self? For it sounds as if it had all leaked out of you, leaked into the universe.

Post-mortem effects. The individuality had leaked out of him.

No, no, don't lay this down to poetry. These are post-mortem effects. And Walt's great poems are really huge fat tomb-plants, great rank graveyard growths.

All that false exuberance. All those lists of things boiled in one pudding-cloth! No, no!

I don't want all those things inside me, thank you.

"I reject nothing," says Walt.

If that is so, one must be a pipe open at both ends, so everything runs through.

Post-mortem effects.

"I embrace ALL," says Whitman. "I weave all things into myself."

Do you really! There can't be much left of *you* when you've done. When you've cooked the awful pudding of One Identity.

"And whoever walks a furlong without sympathy walks to his own funeral dressed in his own shroud."

Take off your hat then, my funeral procession of one is passing.

This awful Whitman. This post-mortem poet. This poet with the private soul leaking out of him all the time. All his privacy leaking out in a sort of dribble, oozing into the universe.

Walt becomes in his own person the whole world, the whole universe, the whole eternity of time, as far as his rather sketchy knowledge of history will carry him, that is. Because to *be* a thing he had to know it. In order to assume the identity of a thing he had to know that thing. He was not able to assume one identity with Charlie Chaplin, for example, because Walt didn't know Charlie. What a pity! He'd have done poems, pæans and what not, Chants, Songs of Cinematernity.

"Oh, Charlie, my Charlie, another film is done——"

As soon as Walt *knew* a thing, he assumed a One Identity with it. If he knew that an Eskimo sat in a kyak, immediately there was Walt being little and yellow and greasy, sitting in a kyak.

Now will you tell me exactly what a kyak is?

Who is he that demands petty definition? Let him behold me *sitting in a kyak*.

I behold no such thing. I behold a rather fat old man full of a rather senile, self-conscious sensuosity.

DEMOCRACY. EN MASSE. ONE IDENTITY.

The universe is short, adds up to ONE.

ONE.

I.

Which is Walt.

His poems, *Democracy*, *En Masse*, *One Identity*, they are long sums in addition and multiplication, of which the answer is invariably MYSELF.

He reaches the state of ALLNESS.

And what then? It's all empty. Just an empty Allness. An addled egg.

Walt wasn't an Eskimo. A little, yellow, sly, cunning, greasy little Eskimo. And when Walt blandly assumed Allness, including Eskimoness, unto himself, he was just sucking the wind out of a blown egg-shell, no more. Eskimos are not minor little Walts. They are something that I am not, I know that. Outside the egg of my Allness chuckles the greasy little Eskimo. Outside the egg of Whitman's Allness too.

But Walt wouldn't have it. He was everything and everything was in him. He drove an automobile with a very fierce headlight, along the track of a fixed idea, through the darkness of this world. And he saw everything that way. Just as a motorist does in the night.

I, who happen to be asleep under the bushes in the dark, hoping a snake won't crawl into my neck; I, seeing Walt go by in his great fierce poetic machine, think to myself: What a funny world that fellow sees!

ONE DIRECTION! toots Walt in the car, whizzing along it.

Whereas there are myriads of ways in the dark, not to mention trackless wildernesses, as anyone will know who cares to come off the road—even the Open Road.

ONE DIRECTION! whoops America, and sets off also in an automobile.

ALLNESS! shrieks Walt at a cross-road, going whizz over an unwary Red Indian.

ONE IDENTITY! chants democratic En Masse, pelting behind in motor-cars, oblivious of the corpses under the wheels.

God save me, I feel like creeping down a rabbit-hole, to get away from all these automobiles rushing down the ONE IDENTITY track to the goal of ALLNESS.

"A woman waits for me——"

He might as well have said: "The femaleness waits for my maleness." Oh, beautiful generalization and abstraction! Oh, biological function.

"Athletic mothers of these States——" Muscles and wombs. They needn't have had faces at all.

"As I see myself reflected in Nature,
  As I see through a mist, One with inexpressible com-
    pleteness, sanity, beauty,
  See the bent head, and arms folded over the breast, the
    Female I see."

Everything was female to him: even himself. Nature just one great function.

"This is the nucleus—after the child is born of woman,
    man is born of woman,
  This is the bath of birth, the merge of small and large,
    and the outlet again——"

"The Female I see——"
If I'd been one of his women, I'd have given him Female, with a flea in his ear.
Always wanting to merge himself into the womb of something or other.
"The Female I see——"
Anything, so long as he could merge himself.
Just a horror. A sort of white flux.
Post-mortem effects.
He found, as all men find, that you can't really merge in a woman, though you may go a long way. You can't manage the last bit. So you have to give it up, and try elsewhere if you *insist* on merging.
In *Calamus* he changes his tune. He doesn't shout and thump and exult any more. He begins to hesitate, reluctant, wistful.
The strange calamus has its pink-tinged root by the pond, and it sends up its leaves of comradeship, comrades from one root, without the intervention of woman, the female.
So he sings of the mystery of manly love, the love of comrades. Over and over he says the same thing: the new world will be built on the love of comrades, the new great dynamic of life will be manly love. Out of this manly love will come the inspiration for the future.
Will it though? Will it?
Comradeship! Comrades! This is to be the new Demo-cracy of Comrades. This is the new cohering principle in the world: Comradeship.
Is it? Are you sure?

It is the cohering principle of true soldiery, we are told in *Drum Taps*. It is the cohering principle in the new unison for creative activity. And it is extreme and alone, touching the confines of death. Something terrible to bear, terrible to be responsible for. Even Walt Whitman felt it. The soul's last and most poignant responsibility, the responsibility of comradeship, of manly love.

> "Yet you are beautiful to me, you faint-tinged roots, you make me think of death.
> Death is beautiful from you (what indeed is finally beautiful except death and love?)
> I think it is not for life I am chanting here my chant of lovers, I think it must be for death,
> For how calm, how solemn it grows to ascend to the atmosphere of lovers,
> Death or life, I am then indifferent, my soul declines to prefer
> (I am not sure but the high soul of lovers welcomes death most)
> Indeed, O death, I think now these leaves mean precisely the same as you mean——"

This is strange, from the exultant Walt.
Death!
Death is now his chant! Death!
Merging! And Death! Which is the final merge.
The great merge into the womb. Woman.
And after that, the merge of comrades: man-for-man love.
And almost immediately with this, death, the final merge of death.
There you have the progression of merging. For the great mergers, woman at last becomes inadequate. For those who love to extremes. Woman is inadequate for the last merging. So the next step is the merging of man-for-man love. And this is on the brink of death. It slides over into death.
David and Jonathan. And the death of Jonathan.
It always slides into death.
The love of comrades.
Merging.
So that if the new Democracy is to be based on the love of comrades, it will be based on death too. It will slip so soon into death.

The last merging. The last Democracy. The last love. The love of comrades.

Fatality. And fatality.

Whitman would not have been the great poet he is if he had not taken the last steps and looked over into death. Death, the last merging, that was the goal of his manhood.

To the mergers, there remains the brief love of comrades, and then Death.

> "Whereto answering, the sea
> Delaying not, hurrying not
> Whispered me through the night, very plainly before
>   daybreak,
> Lisp'd to me the low and delicious word death.
> And again death, death, death, death.
> Hissing melodions, neither like the bird nor like my
>   arous'd child's heart,
> But edging near as privately for me rustling at my feet,
> Creeping thence steadily up to my ears and laving me
>   softly all over,
> Death, death, death, death, death——"

Whitman is a very great poet, of the end of life. A very great post-mortem poet, of the transitions of the soul as it loses its integrity. The poet of the soul's last shout and shriek, on the confines of death. *Après moi le déluge.*

But we have all got to die, and disintegrate.

We have got to die in life, too, and disintegrate while we live.

But even then the goal is not death.

Something else will come.

> "Out of the cradle endlessly rocking."

We've got to die first, anyhow. And disintegrate while we still live.

Only we know this much: Death is not the *goal*. And Love, and merging, are now only part of the death-process. Comradeship—part of the death-process. Democracy—part of the death-process. The new Democracy—the brink of death. One Identity—death itself.

We have died, and we are still disintegrating.

But IT IS FINISHED.

Consummatum est.

Whitman, the great poet, has meant so much to me. Whitman, the one man breaking a way ahead. Whitman, the one pioneer. And only Whitman. No English pioneers, no French. No European pioneer-poets. In Europe the would-be pioneers are mere innovators. The same in America. Ahead of Whitman, nothing. Ahead of all poets, pioneering into the wilderness of unopened life, Whitman. Beyond him, none. His wide, strange camp at the end of the great high-road. And lots of new little poets camping on Whitman's camping ground now. But none going really beyond. Because Whitman's camp is at the end of the road, and on the edge of a great precipice. Over the precipice, blue distances, and the blue hollow of the future. But there is no way down. It is a dead end.

Pisgah. Pisgah sights. And Death. Whitman like a strange, modern, American Moses. Fearfully mistaken. And yet the great leader.

The essential function of art is moral. Not æsthetic, not decorative, not pastime and recreation. But moral. The essential function of art is moral.

But a passionate, implicit morality, not didactic. A morality which changes the blood, rather than the mind. Changes the blood first. The mind follows later, in the wake.

Now Whitman was a great moralist. He was a great leader. He was a great changer of the blood in the veins of men.

Surely it is especially true of American art, that it is all essentially moral. Hawthorne, Poe, Longfellow, Emerson, Melville: it is the moral issue which engages them. They all feel uneasy about the old morality. Sensuously, passionally, they all attack the old morality. But they know nothing better, mentally. Therefore they give tight mental allegiance to a morality which all their passion goes to destroy. Hence the duplicity which is the fatal flaw in them: most fatal in the most perfect American work of art, *The Scarlet Letter*. Tight mental allegiance given to a morality which the passional self repudiates.

Whitman was the first to break the mental allegiance. He was the first to smash the old moral conception that the soul of man is something "superior" and "above" the flesh. Even Emerson still maintained this tiresome "superiority" of the soul. Even Melville could not get over it. Whitman was the first heroic seer to seize the soul by the scruff of her neck and plant her down among the potsherds.

"There!" he said to the soul. "Stay there!"

Stay there. Stay in the flesh. Stay in the limbs and lips and in the belly. Stay in the breast and womb. Stay there, Oh Soul, where you belong.

Stay in the dark limbs of negroes. Stay in the body of the prostitute. Stay in the sick flesh of the syphilitic. Stay in the marsh where the calamus grows. Stay there, Soul, where you belong.

The Open Road. The great home of the Soul is the open road. Not heaven, not paradise. Not "above". Not even "within". The soul is neither "above" nor "within". It is a wayfarer down the open road.

Not by meditating. Not by fasting. Not by exploring heaven after heaven, inwardly, in the manner of the great mystics. Not by exaltation. Not by ecstasy. Not by any of these ways does the soul come into her own.

Only by taking the open road.

Not through charity. Not through sacrifice. Not even through love. Not through good works. Not through these does the soul accomplish herself.

Only through the journey down the open road.

The journey itself, down the open road. Exposed to full contact. On two slow feet. Meeting whatever comes down the open road. In company with those that drift in the same measure along the same way. Towards no goal. Always the open road.

Having no known direction even. Only the soul remaining true to herself in her going.

Meeting all the other wayfarers along the road. And how? How meet them, and how pass? With sympathy, says Whitman. Sympathy. He does not say love. He says sympathy. Feeling with. Feel with them as they feel with themselves. Catching the vibration of their soul and flesh as we pass.

It is a new great doctrine. A doctrine of life. A new great morality. A morality of actual living, not of salvation. Europe has never got beyond the morality of salvation. America to this day is deathly sick with saviourism. But Whitman, the greatest and the first and the only American teacher, was no Saviour. His morality was no morality of salvation. His was a morality of the soul living her life, not saving herself. Accepting the contact with other souls along the open way, as they lived their lives. Never trying to save them. As lief try to arrest them and throw them in gaol. The soul living her life along the incarnate mystery of the open road.

This was Whitman. And the true rhythm of the American continent speaking out in him. He is the first white aboriginal.

"In my Father's house are many mansions."

"No," said Whitman. "Keep out of mansions. A mansion may be heaven on earth, but you might as well be dead. Strictly avoid mansions. The soul is herself when she is going on foot down the open road."

It is the American heroic message. The soul is not to pile up defences round herself. She is not to withdraw and seek her heavens inwardly, in mystical ecstasies. She is not to cry to some God beyond, for salvation. She is to go down the open road, as the road opens, into the unknown, keeping company with those whose soul draws them near to her, accomplishing nothing save the journey, and the works incident to the journey, in the long life-travel into the unknown, the soul in her subtle sympathies accomplishing herself by the way.

This is Whitman's essential message. The heroic message of the American future. It is the inspiration of thousands of Americans to-day, the best souls of to-day, men and women. And it is a message that only in America can be fully understood, finally accepted.

Then Whitman's mistake. The mistake of his interpretation of his watchword: Sympathy. The mystery of SYMPATHY. He still confounded it with Jesus' LOVE, and with Paul's CHARITY. Whitman, like all the rest of us, was at the end of the great emotional highway of Love. And because he couldn't help himself, he carried on his Open Road as a prolongation of the emotional highway of Love, beyond Calvary. The highway of Love ends at the foot of the Cross. There is no beyond. It was a hopeless attempt to prolong the highway of love.

He didn't follow his Sympathy. Try as he might, he kept on automatically interpreting it as Love, as Charity. Merging!

This merging, *en masse*, One Identity, Myself monomania was a carry-over from the old Love idea. It was carrying the idea of Love to its logical physical conclusion. Like Flaubert and the leper. The decree of unqualified Charity, as the soul's one means of salvation, still in force.

Now Whitman wanted his soul to save itself; *he* didn't want to save it. Therefore he did not need the great Christian receipt for saving the soul. He needed to supersede the Christian Charity, the Christian Love, within himself, in order to give his Soul her last freedom. The high-road of Love is no Open Road. It is a narrow, tight way, where the soul walks hemmed in between compulsions.

Whitman wanted to take his Soul down the open road. And he failed in so far as he failed to get out of the old rut of Salvation. He forced his Soul to the edge of a cliff, and he looked down into death. And there he camped, powerless. He had carried out his Sympathy as an extension of Love and Charity. And it had brought him almost to madness and soul-death. It gave him. his forced, unhealthy, post-mortem quality.

His message was really the opposite of Henley's rant:

> "I am the master of my fate,
> I am the captain of my soul."

Whitman's essential message was the Open Road. The leaving of the soul free unto herself, the leaving of his fate to her and to the loom of the open road. Which is the bravest doctrine man has ever proposed to himself.

Alas, he didn't quite carry it out. He couldn't quite break the old maddening bond of the love-compulsion; he couldn't quite get out of the rut of the charity habit—for Love and Charity have degenerated now into habit: a bad habit.

Whitman said Sympathy. If only he had stuck to it! Because Sympathy means feeling with, not feeling for. He kept on having a passionate feeling *for* the negro slave, or the prostitute, or the syphilitic—which is merging. A sinking of Walt Whitman's soul in the souls of these others.

He wasn't keeping to his open road. He was forcing his soul down an old rut. He wasn't leaving her free. He was forcing her into other people's circumstances.

Supposing he had felt true sympathy with the negro

slave? He would have felt *with* the negro slave. Sympathy
—compassion—which is partaking of the passion which
was in the soul of the negro slave.

What was the feeling in the negro's soul?

"Ah, I am a slave! Ah, it is bad to be a slave! I must
free myself. My soul will die unless she frees herself. My
soul says I must free myself."

Whitman came along, and saw the slave, and said to
himself: "That negro slave is a man like myself. We share
the same identity. And he is bleeding with wounds. Oh,
oh, is it not myself who am also bleeding with wounds?"

This was not *sympathy*. It was merging and self-sacrifice.
"Bear ye one another's burdens": "Love thy neighbour
as thyself": "Whatsoever ye do unto him, ye do unto
me."

If Whitman had truly *sympathized*, he would have said:
"That negro slave suffers from slavery. He wants to free
himself. His soul wants to free him. He has wounds, but
they are the price of freedom. The soul has a long journey
from slavery to freedom. If I can help him I will: I will
not take over his wounds and his slavery to myself. But I
will help him fight the power that enslaves him when he
wants to be free, if he wants my help, since I see in his
face that he needs to be free. But even when he is free, his
soul has many journeys down the open road, before it is
a free soul."

And of the prostitute Whitman would have said:

"Look at that prostitute! Her nature has turned evil
under her mental lust for prostitution. She has lost her
soul. She knows it herself. She likes to make men lose their
souls. If she tried to make me lose my soul, I would kill
her. I wish she may die."

But of another prostitute he would have said:

"Look! She is fascinated by the Priapic mysteries. Look,
she will soon by worn to death by the Priapic usage. It is
the way of her soul. She wishes it so."

Of the syphilitic he would say:

"Look! She wants to infect all men with syphilis. We
ought to kill her."

And of still another syphilitic:

"Look! She has a horror of her syphilis. If she looks my
way I will help her to get cured."

This is sympathy. The soul judging for herself, and preserving her own integrity.

But when, in Flaubert, the man takes the leper to his naked body; when Bubi de Montparnasse takes the girl because he knows she's got syphilis; when Whitman embraces an evil prostitute: that is not sympathy. The evil prostitute has no desire to be embraced with love; so if you sympathize with her, you won't try to embrace her with love. The leper loathes his leprosy, so if you sympathize with him, you'll loathe it too. The evil woman who wishes to infect all men with her syphilis hates you if you haven't got syphilis. If you sympathize, you'll feel her hatred, and you'll hate too, you'll hate her. Her feeling is hate, and you'll share it. Only your soul will choose the direction of its own hatred.

The soul is a very perfect judge of her own motions, if your mind doesn't dictate to her. Because the mind says Charity! Charity! you don't have to force your soul into kissing lepers or embracing syphilitics. Your lips are the lips of your soul, your body is the body of your soul; your own single, individual soul. That is Whitman's message. And your soul hates syphilis and leprosy. Because it *is* a soul, it hates these things, which are against the soul. And therefore to force the body of your soul into contact with uncleanness is a great violation of your soul. The soul wishes to keep clean and whole. The soul's deepest will is to preserve its own integrity, against the mind and the whole mass of disintegrating forces.

Soul sympathizes with soul. And that which tries to kill my soul, my soul hates. My soul and my body are one. Soul and body wish to keep clean and whole. Only the mind is capable of great perversion. Only the mind tries to drive my soul and body into uncleanness and unwholesomeness.

What my soul loves, I love.

What my soul hates, I hate.

When my soul is stirred with compassion, I am compassionate.

What my soul turns away from, I turn away from.

That is the *true* interpretation of Whitman's creed: the true revelation of his Sympathy.

And my soul takes the open road. She meets the souls

that are passing, she goes along with the souls that are going her way. And for one and all, she has sympathy. The sympathy of love, the sympathy of hate, the sympathy of simple proximity; all the subtle sympathizings of the incalculable soul, from the bitterest hate to passionate love.

It is not I who guide my soul to heaven. It is I who am guided by my own soul along the open road, where all men tread. Therefore, I must accept her deep motions of love, or hate, or compassion, or dislike, or indifference. And I must go where she takes me, for my feet and my lips and my body are my soul. It is I who must submit to her.

This is Whitman's message of American democracy.

The true democracy, where soul meets soul, in the open road. Democracy. American democracy where all journey down the open road, and where a soul is known at once in its going. Not by its clothes or appearance. Whitman did away with that. Not by its family name. Not even by its reputation. Whitman and Melville both discounted that. Not by a progression of piety, or by works of Charity. Not by works at all. Not by anything, but just itself. The soul passing unenhanced, passing on foot and being no more than itself. And recognized, and passed by or greeted according to the soul's dictate. If it be a great soul, it will be worshipped in the road.

The love of man and woman: a recognition of souls, and a communion of worship. The love of comrades: a recognition of souls, and a communion of worship. Democracy: a recognition of souls, all down the open road, and a great soul seen in its greatness, as it travels on foot among the rest, down the common way of the living. A glad recognition of souls, and a gladder worship of great and greater souls, because they are the only riches.

Love, and Merging, brought Whitman to the Edge of Death! Death! Death!

But the exultance of his message still remains. Purified of MERGING, purified of MYSELF, the exultant message of American Democracy, of souls in the Open Road, full of glad recognition, full of fierce readiness, full of the joy of worship, when one soul sees a greater soul.

The only riches, the great souls.